Cybersecurity Incident Response

How to Contain, Eradicate, and Recover from Incidents

Eric C. Thompson

Apress®

Cybersecurity Incident Response: How to Contain, Eradicate, and Recover from Incidents

Eric C. Thompson
Lisle, Illinois, USA

ISBN-13 (pbk): 978-1-4842-3869-1 ISBN-13 (electronic): 978-1-4842-3870-7
https://doi.org/10.1007/978-1-4842-3870-7

Library of Congress Control Number: 2018957666

Managing Director, Apress Media LLC: Welmoed Spahr
Acquisitions Editor: Susan McDermott
Development Editor: Laura Berendson
Coordinating Editor: Rita Fernando

Cover designed by eStudioCalamar

Distributed to the book trade worldwide by Springer Science+Business Media New York, 233 Spring Street, 6th Floor, New York, NY 10013. Phone 1-800-SPRINGER, fax (201) 348-4505, e-mail orders-ny@springer-sbm.com, or visit www.springeronline.com. Apress Media, LLC is a California LLC and the sole member (owner) is Springer Science + Business Media Finance Inc (SSBM Finance Inc). SSBM Finance Inc is a **Delaware** corporation.

For information on translations, please e-mail rights@apress.com, or visit http://www.apress.com/rights-permissions.

Apress titles may be purchased in bulk for academic, corporate, or promotional use. eBook versions and licenses are also available for most titles. For more information, reference our Print and eBook Bulk Sales web page at http://www.apress.com/bulk-sales.

Any source code or other supplementary material referenced by the author in this book is available to readers on GitHub via the book's product page, located at www.apress.com/9781484238691. For more detailed information, please visit http://www.apress.com/source-code.

Printed on acid-free paper

Table of Contents

About the Author

Eric C. Thompson is an accomplished governance, risk, and compliance professional. As of Director of Information Security and Compliance at Blue Health Intelligence (BHI), Eric leads efforts to increase cyber security maturity in several domains, including governance, policy and controls, risk management, cyber security strategy, and business alignment. He established the risk management function which includes assessment, analysis and treatments of risks, threat and vulnerability management strategy, and due diligence requirements for assessing third-party risk. In his new role, Eric added cybersecurity operations and incident response to his list of responsibilities. Both are now information security passions.

Prior to BHI, Eric spent seven years at Ernst & Young in the Advisory practice where he specialized in helping healthcare organizations (providers, payers, and business associates) solve problems related to information security, risk management, and compliance when dealing with electronic medical records. Eric led the HITRUST Common Security Framework (CSF) cybersecurity program management and third-party risk management assessments.

Eric is also a proud member of the SANS Mentor team.

About the Technical Reviewer

Andrew Reeder serves as the HIPAA (Health Insurance Portability and Accountability Act of 1996) security officer and director of HIPAA Privacy at Rush University Medical Center, a major academic medical center in Chicago. In this role, Andy provides leadership in achieving regulatory compliance related to information-protection requirements, with major responsibilities including response and investigation into HIPAA privacy and security incidents, coordination of patient privacy rights actions, and policy development. Andy also serves as an adjunct faculty member in the College of Computing and Digital Media at DePaul University, where he teaches cybersecurity and information assurance topics at the graduate and undergraduate levels. Andy has been involved in providing privacy and information security services for many years and has previously served as director, Information Security, for a major Chicago-area regional healthcare provider and as a senior manager at a major professional services firm. He holds CISSP, CISA, CISM, CHPC, and HCISPP certifications and a master's degree in public administration.

Acknowledgments

Again, I want to thank Susan McDermott and Rita Fernando for making this project come to life. Also, thank you to Andy Reeder for his help as technical editor.

Introduction

There are two reasons I wrote this book. The first, I've sat through several incident response table-top exercises and witnessed firsthand how uncomfortable the process is when one does not feel prepared. Second, I read Urban Meyer's book above the line, which I felt spoke to me about how to create a culture of preparation, teamwork and no excuses.

This book is not a technical book with deep dives into incident response forensics. You will not learn how to perform and analyze memory dumps here. This work focuses on how to establish an incident response program. It focuses on policy, strategy, people and process. It was written for members of incident response teams building and enhancing the program and for executives and members of management. Stakeholder in incident response not part of IT can read this book and get a sense of what the incident response program should look like.

This book begins by discussing the need for strong incident response capabilities. In this current landscape, cybersecurity programs are judged by the ability to respond to incidents. Necessary protective capabilities must exist and a framework for responding to incidents established. Leadership qualities, strategy development and pre-planning are covered. Each phase of incident response: identification, containment, eradication and recovery are outlined in detail before discussion how to monitor the program using NIST 800-137 is presented.

The book is ends with a story about an incident designed to show how unplanned and unfocused responses leads to worse outcomes.

The reader is left with thoughts on how take action toward building and enhancing the incident response program, and knowledge of how much effort it takes to be successful.

CHAPTER 1

The Significance of Incident Response

Effective incident response forms the criteria used to judge cybersecurity programs. Effective protection and detection measures do not matter if the response to an event falls short. Within days of an announcement, news articles criticizing an entity's response can negatively influence public opinion. Sizable data breaches elicit scrutiny that can last for years. Target became a prime example of this when it suffered a breach in 2014, and Equifax reinforced this fact in 2017. Criticism for not communicating news of the breach and possessing all the answers nagged both entities early in the response process. Equifax's subsequent missteps beyond communication issues caused the incident response process to appear ineffective. These perceptions survive long after breach recovery has occurred.

A comprehensive plan that covers every fundamental aspect of incident response, practiced regularly, seems sufficient, until an incident actually occurs. The plan and the skills practiced can be forgotten. Individuals can panic, freeze, and fail to make decisions; others become cowboys, expecting to save the day. The hard truth remains: perceived cybersecurity program success lives and dies with effective detection, containment, eradication, and recovery from security incidents. Initial reports and public scrutiny seem to center on how long it takes entities to disclose incidents.

Information security blogger Brian Krebs broke the news of the Target breach,[1] causing the retailer to lose its ability to control and manage messaging of the event. Equifax experienced the same issues. These included accusations made against

---

[1]KrebsOnSecurity, "Sources: Target Investigating Data Breach," https://krebsonsecurity.com/2013/12/sources-target-investigating-data-breach/, December 18, 2013.

executives, victims directed to vulnerable web sites, and speculation that the same attackers breached Equifax months earlier, casting a long shadow over Equifax's response to the breach.[2,3]

Why Does This Happen?

Incident response is the face of an entity's cybersecurity program. This places a strong emphasis on the need for an effective response program.

Why do so many incident responses fall short of the mark? There are several reasons, which are shown in Table 1-1.

Table 1-1. *Common Themes Found in Ineffective Incident Response Plans*

Cause	Details
Lack of Planning	The incident response plan and playbooks are inadequate, missing key processes and actions.
Lack of Preparation	Effective incident response requires muscle memory. Continuously referring to the response plan, trying to find the correct steps in playbooks, and not knowing what steps are necessary because specific scenarios were not anticipated lead to failure.
Lack of Leadership	The program requires effective leadership on the team and from management. Individuals who panic and lose their cool in the heat of battle do little to forge an effective response.
Lack of Management Support	Response teams cannot second-guess themselves during an incident. If taking systems offline is the necessary action then senior management criticizing such actions because it possibly affected the business does not demonstrate strong backing by management.

Incident response programs require prioritization within the overall cybersecurity program and management must view incident response as an important business function. This means doing more than writing an incident response plan and conducting

---

[2]KrebsOnSecurity, "Equifax Breach Response Turns Dumpster Fire," https://krebsonsecurity.com/2017/09/equifax-breach-response-turns-dumpster-fire/, September 8, 2017.

[3]KrebsOnSecurity, "Equifax Breach: Setting the Record Straight," https://krebsonsecurity.com/2017/09/equifax-breach-setting-the-record-straight/, September 20, 2017.

a tabletop exercise once a year. Operating as a program means that incident response undergoes continuous review and improvement on a regular basis. The plan must be fluid, and each event, incident, and breach responded to is an opportunity for analysis of what went well and what opportunities for improvement exist. Frequent testing of the program and its processes yield beneficial feedback. A road map outlining the trajectory of the incident response program, from initial development to mature program backed by effective processes, drives annual projects and actions.

While laying the groundwork for the program the members of the team must prepare themselves. There is no substitute for practice. Reviewing your risk analysis, documenting other breaches, and referring to resources such as Mandiant's Attack Life Cycle make it easy to generate practice scenarios. I am not talking about high-tech practice. The team picks a scenario and then walks through the process of analysis, triage, and response. At the end of each walkthrough, the team identifies what works and what does not and adds missing pieces in the response playbooks.

Leadership might be third on the list, but gaps in leadership skills often derail any hope for an effective response. In the worst case, poor leadership causes less significant events to create more damage than expected. Figure 1-1 displays components of an effective incident response program that leaders must establish. Jim Collins, in his book *Good to Great*, outlined these items as areas of strategic importance to any program or entity.

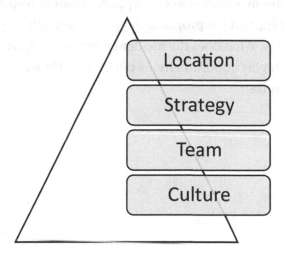

Figure 1-1. *Components of an incident response program developed those leading the response*

Leaders start by defining the culture of the organization they direct. This applies to the incident response program too. In Chapter 5, an in-depth review of culture and its importance to success illustrates how culturally defined behaviors are meant to lead the program toward success. Leaders begin by getting the right people on the team.[4] Choosing the incident response team consists of more than selecting the smartest or most technically gifted individuals. Team members aligned with the goals, objectives, and cultural expectations prove more valuable than technically gifted individuals, if the latter do not buy into the program's goals and objectives.[5] Once culture and team requirements are established, the strategy to meet the program's goal—to detect, contain, eradicate, recover, and assess lessons learned quickly, while minimizing damage to the entity—requires individuals with specific talents. If those talents do not exist internally, strategic partnerships must be established with external parties. This gap is not identifiable until the team is created. This strategic element is not defined until the team is identified. In *Good to Great*, Collins defines location as the need for businesses to know where they want to compete. This also applies to incident response. Will key incident response processes remain on-premise or off-premise? Will they be executed by a third party? Small and medium-size organizations often lack the resources to execute all elements of an incident response internally. Large organizations also rely heavily on outside professionals for vital incident response processes.

The last critical element is management support. Incident response fails when management does not support the program. Support is not only required during an incident but every day. What does the incident response program require from management? Several highly important items outlined in Figure 1-2 illustrate the daily nature of incident response.

---

[4]Jim Collins, *Good to Great* (New York: Harper Collins, 2001).
[5]Urban Meyer, *Above the Line* (New York: Penguin Books, 2015).

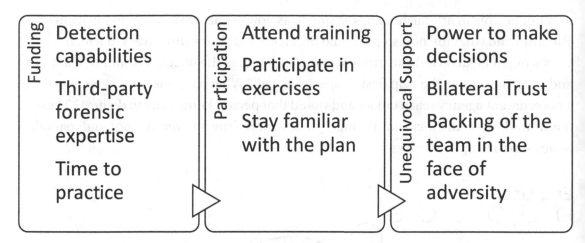

Figure 1-2. *The incident response program's requirements, from left to right, are dependent on the factors in the preceding box*

The first box in Figure 1-2 emphasizes funding. Without money, an incident response program cannot function. The program requires the best possible detection and response capabilities the budget can sustain. Capabilities include technical components and people to establish and maintain key processes. Data loss prevention (DLP), end point detection and response (EDR), and the ability to capture full packets, stream headers, headers, and net flow traffic are examples of technological capabilities. Entities of all sizes use third parties to conduct forensic investigations. These entities bring their own tools into the environment. The more evidence available for the forensic team to analyze, the better. The last funding element is time. Program participants need time to practice the following:

- Technical first responders must rehearse responses to varying incident types and make improvements to playbooks.

- Leaders must rehearse scenarios and evaluate decision making.

- The executive team must rehearse how it takes in information, evaluates the scenario, and makes decisions.

Practice takes time. Achieving desired results requires a significant time commitment. Many practice sessions are necessary to instill the ability to respond appropriately without overthinking. An annual or semiannual tabletop exercise does not suffice. The objective is to ensure that response plan tactics are ingrained in the team, so certain actions become automatic. Without focused practice, incident responders may not be able to articulate things as simple as how events are brought to the team's attention and what the next steps should be. Figure 1-3 shows three ways in which events might be detected and brought to the attention of the incident response team. Do end-user alerts go to the help desk or special e-mail? What happens next? Who would a government agency reach out to, and would that person know what to do next? These questions kick off the incident response process, and if the answers are not understood, issues slip through the cracks.

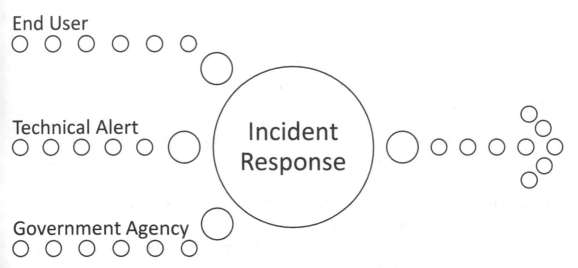

Figure 1-3. *Three common ways events and incidents may be detected*

End-user reporting, monitoring tools, and government agencies are common sources of alerts. It is not unusual for the Federal Bureau of Investigation (FBI) to uncover evidence of a potential breach when investigating other intrusions. No matter the source of the alert, team members must be able to triage the situation and know automatically the next step in the process. These actions must be intentional, purposeful, and skillful.[6] There is no room for ad hoc behavior that does not follow the plan. This applies to executives as well. The executive team must attend all training, participate in training exercises, and keep abreast of the plan.

---

[6]Urban Meyer, *Above the Line* (New York: Penguin Books, 2015).

Strategy vs. Tactics

When incident response is led by technical individuals, the program risks getting bogged down in tactical details and misses the need for a clear strategy. The incident response plan is built on a strategy of detection, containment, and eradication of intrusions and infections before impact to sensitive data and/or business operations. Figures 1-4 and 1-5 display two ways to express this concept. Strategies are built around the assets of concern, thinking through risks and attack scenarios likely to occur. Included in the analysis are fundamental protection and prevention capabilities, not just detection and response measures. These measures are built around use cases and derived from the attack scenarios identified, to deploy resources and build the strategic objectives of the incident response plan.

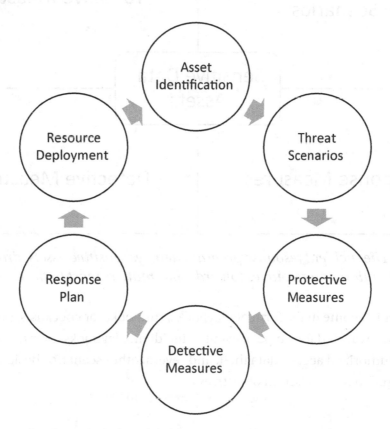

Figure 1-4. *Cyclical approach to building a strategic response plan*

Continuous analysis and review take place through practice exercises and reviewing actual events. New threats or intelligence about an attacker's processes, tactics, and techniques (PPTs) and indicators of compromise (IOCs) push the team to analyze this data in terms of affected assets. The team must understand if the protective, detective, and response capabilities are adequate. If not, alternative or compensating processes must fill the void.

Figure 1-5 presents an illustration of how the cybersecurity program and, specifically, the incident response program are deployed around sensitive assets.

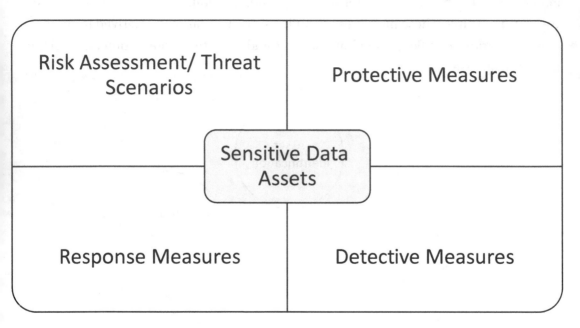

Figure 1-5. *The incident response program deploys sensitive assets, drawing the program's attention and resources toward what matters most to the organization*

Tactics, which come in the form of playbooks, runbooks, or checklists, outline the specific actions expected for a type of event or incident. Playbooks for ransomware, malware, unauthorized access, data theft, and several other scenarios designate specific actions required to meet program objectives.

Changing the Culture

To achieve the goal of building an effective incident response program, changes in how senior management, information technology, and cybersecurity personnel think about incident response may be necessary. Annual testing and remediation as an approach to response preparation is considered sufficient. This approach is used by most entities today. Auditors and regulators also accept this approach when assessing entities. Cybersecurity auditors consider this sufficient and rarely challenge auditees on this notion.

Senior management must embrace incident response as a program vital to organization objectives and support it with the necessary resources and commitment. Too often, the C-Suite does not consider cyber/information security as anything more than a cost function or necessary evil. Despite increased accountability and scrutiny in the face of breaches and breach response, little seems to change.

To combat these challenges, effective organizational change management is necessary.

Note   If responding to an incident drives public perception of the entity and its ability to act responsibly, shouldn't executives invest the time necessary to make the incident response program successful?

Several models and approaches exist to aid the drive of organizational change and achieve buy-in from the internal stakeholders with the influence necessary to make the program successful. These models are discussed in greater detail in Chapter 3.

Summary

Effective incident response defines how outsiders, the media, regulators, customers, and the public view the competence of the cybersecurity team and the entity. When incident response programs fail, it is for several reasons, mainly a lack of

- Leadership
- Preparation
- Execution

Leadership is the number-one need and driver of successful incident response. Leaders must ensure that the right people are part of the response team, create a culture focused on the necessary behaviors leading to success, and keep calm in the face of a storm. Leaders cannot lose control of emotions, allow team members to act outside of their role on the team and deviate from the incident response plan.

There must be consistent practice, ranging from full-blown tabletop exercises to smaller scenarios using specific playbooks. The goal is to develop muscle memory, helping team members to get comfortable with their roles and instilling confidence in their ability to respond appropriately.

Migration from traditional approaches to incident response, which centers on annual tabletop exercises, requires change in how the organization thinks about incident response and preparation. Effectively changing behaviors toward incident response across all members of the entity is the most important success factor for incident response.

CHAPTER 2

Necessary Prerequisites

Prior to building the incident response program, specific capabilities must exist. At a minimum, these should include adoption of a chosen framework; an understanding of the assets the entity must focus on protecting; documentation of the risks to the confidentiality, integrity, and availability of the assets; and assurance that all fundamental protective capabilities exist. Examples of these capabilities include:

- Access-control processes and restriction of elevated privileges

- Protection from misuse of data in motion, in use, and at rest

- Hardening of hardware, based on established standards

- Understanding and management of vulnerabilities

- Existence of communication and control network protections (firewalls, etc.)

Establishing the Identify and Protect Functions

Cybersecurity is a cost function, one not viewed as a driver of revenue for an organization. Rarely does the information security program get noticed when things are going well. Cybersecurity leaders must continually justify a program's expense and need for full-time employees (FTEs). A business may never see value in cybersecurity until a crisis is averted or mitigated successfully. More likely, security gets blamed when a breach occurs. Despite these challenges, cybersecurity must work through these challenges to protect an entity's assets. The first step is to define the cybersecurity program through the National Institute of Standards and Technology (NIST) Cybersecurity Framework (CSF), as outlined in Figure 2-1, by creating a strategy aligned with the NIST CSF:

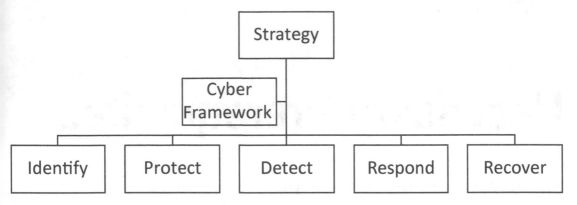

Figure 2-1. *Components of the cybersecurity program required to build a highly effective response program*

Defined Cybersecurity Program

To achieve the goal of incident response, which is to mitigate the impact of events, incidents, and breaches, the entire cybersecurity program must operate effectively, not just the response and recovery programs. The program should be driven by purpose and mission, communicated to all members of the cybersecurity team, which, in turn, should be aligned and working toward the same objectives.

> *Cybersecurity shall relentlessly protect our patient's health information by establishing effective, fundamental Identify and Protect capabilities and building world-class Detect, Response and Recover capabilities.*

This healthcare provider example of a mission statement also describes the strategy for protecting patient information. The mission and purpose are to relentlessly protect patient information, and the strategy is focused on building fundamental identification and protection capabilities, then world-class detection, response, and recover capabilities. All of the preceding components (see Figure 2-1) are derived from subcategories within the NIST CSF.

After establishing the purpose and mission, the program is assessed and measured to determine the maturity and effectiveness of the current state. Measuring the current state drives the road map for meeting the mission. Using a three-year time horizon, annual objectives push the program forward. Creating accountability for the who, what, where, when, and how of achieving program objectives; forming subprograms; and achieving alignment with the mission come next.

A Programmatic Approach

Building cybersecurity programs leads to measurement and improvement actions that continue year over year. Domain thinking might lead to focusing on competencies and one-and-done approaches for certain capabilities. For example, the Protective Technology subcategory of the NIST CSF Protect category. Implementing firewalls managed by a security engineer could lead some to feel the network perimeter is sufficiently protected. No additional effort is required for this subcategory. Programs are continuous. Iterations, cycles, or sprints (the terms do not matter) occur with defined milestones. Once those milestones are met, new ones are created. In terms of a cybersecurity program, the hope is that milestones become more incremental as the program matures.

Identifying Programs

The Protective Technology subcategory logically fits into a network protection program. The program leader and team should focus on ensuring that fundamental technology is implemented. People and process components keep devices configured according to secure leading practices. Highly mature programs track specific metrics and analyze each according to criteria established by the entity, such as the following: Was traffic blocked incorrectly? Was malicious traffic missed? Were configuration changes made without approval or insecure configurations found? This data is used during annual planning and budget exercises to identify improvements in people, processes, and technology, to make the program more effective. In a program-centric environment, this ritual occurs annually, to ensure that the program remains on track to meet the organization's needs. Figure 2-2 illustrates examples of programs entities may create within the NIST CSF.

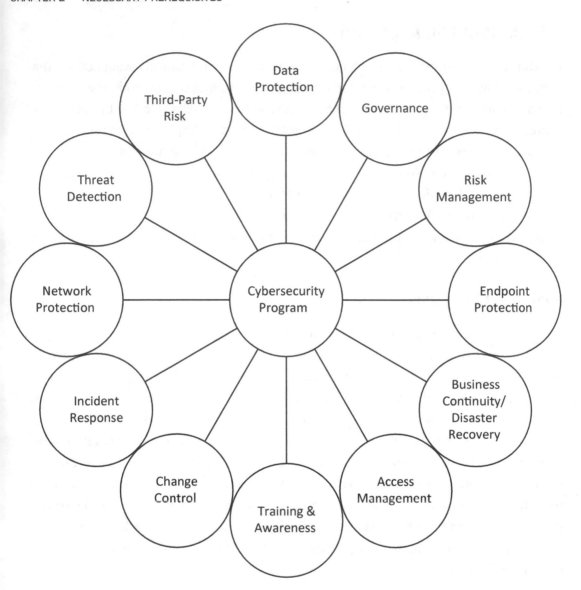

Figure 2-2. *Examples of individual cybersecurity programs within the ABC Cybersecurity Program*

An incident response program is an essential component of a cybersecurity program. Each CSF component serves to make the others better and able to meet the cybersecurity organization's objectives. As outlined earlier in the chapter, an incident response program will not meet its objectives if programs such as access management, data protection, information protection, and all others are not following effective program management.

How Does Each Program Support Incident Response?

Incident response, as a program, is vital to an entity so that damage from attacks is limited. Incident response is not a stand-alone program. Without effective programs supporting it, limited capabilities exist to quickly detect, contain, eradicate, and recover from breaches. Figure 2-3 shows examples of how each program contributes to incident response.

Data Protection
- Establishing baselines for what is "normal" helps first responders and threat hunters to find evidence of an attack.

Governance
- Roles and responsibilities are established, along with expectations of behavior by the user base.

Risk Management
- Documented risks with severity levels guide incident response planning by helping it think through attack scenarios and plan responses to those scenarios.

End point Protection
- Effective end point protection does not only, prevent but detects unusual activities and records events key to investigating attacks.

Business Continuity/Disaster Recovery
- Availability as a security objective is supported by the business-continuity and disaster-recovery programs, facilitating recovery from outages due to attack.

Access Management
- This one is obvious. If access is not controlled, the ability to move laterally and elevate privileges becomes too easy.

Training and Awareness
- End users must know whom to contact if they observe something out of the ordinary.

Change Control
- Limiting who can make changes and restricting how they are made reduces attack vectors.

Network Protection
- Scenarios such as network segmentation complicate attackers' ability to reach their objectives.

Threat Protection
- Keep track of the threat actors and the tactics, techniques, and procedures.

Third-Party Risk
- A strong grasp on how far the entity's boundary extends and where weaknesses exist lessens the burden on investigators.

Figure 2-3. *Examples of how each cybersecurity program within an entity supports incident response. Deficiencies in each program reduce the effectiveness of the incident response program.*

Summary

Prior to acting on the desire to build a best-in-class incident response program, it is necessary to establish the capabilities outlined in the Identify and Protect Functions of the NIST CSF. These NIST CSF functions, as part of cybersecurity programs supporting the incident response program, must be fundamentally effective. Without governance, risk management, asset management, network protection, threat management, access management, change control, training and awareness, and business continuity/disaster recovery, it is nearly impossible for the incident response program to be effective. Each of the programs outlined executes key activities required for incident response to be effective. Without these, the potential for incident response to meet the entity's needs is limited.

CHAPTER 3

Incident Response Frameworks

Initiating the construction or assessment of the incident response program requires a blueprint. Leveraging leading practices lessons learned from others shortens the incident response learning curve. The National Institute of Standards and Technology (NIST) publishes many documents available for cybersecurity practitioners, specifically, the NIST (SP) 800-61 Computer Security Incident Handling Guide. The guidance in this document addresses the incident response elements required to build a plan and team. This approach removes the guesswork and prevents the program from becoming purely technical in nature. Cybersecurity events and incidents are not just cybersecurity problems but business problems. Although NIST SPs are designed to ensure compliance by federal agencies, they are considered best practices and often adopted by industry.

The elements of NIST 800-61 include the following:

- Organizing a Computer Incident Response Capability

- Handling an Incident

  - Identify

  - Contain

  - Eradicate

  - Recover

- Post-incident

The design and implementation of these elements are led by the program owner and team. Teams consist of core members, first responders when events occur, and the extended team. Information technology, legal, corporate compliance, and business executives are potential members of the extended team. Once the team is in place, the goals, strategy, and objectives of the incident response program are considered. As discussed in Chapter 2, this process is described by Jim Collins in his book *Good to Great*.[1] It is hoped that entities assessing their incident response programs utilize a cybersecurity program framework as well, such as the NIST Cybersecurity Framework or NIST (SP) 800-53 Security and Privacy Controls for Information Systems and Organizations, because the elements in NIST (SP) 800-61 are meant to be incorporated into the cybersecurity program, processes, and controls.

NIST 800-61[2]

NIST established special publication 800-61 to help federal agencies establish and implement incident response. This document illustrates how incident response capabilities should be established and how incidents should be handled.

Organizing a Computer Incident Response Capability

Organizing an incident response program requires that an incident be defined. Not everything that is unusual is an incident. Prior to defining anomalies as incidents, these occurrences must be analyzed and triaged as events. Criteria for each should be top of mind during the creation of the following:

- Policies and procedures
- The team
- Goals, strategy, and objectives
- The incident response plan
- Tactical procedures

---

[1]Jim Collins, *Good to Great* (New York: Harper Collins, 2001).

[2]Paul Cichonski et al., "Computer Security Incident Handling Guide," NIST Special Publication 800-61, Revision 2, http://nvlpubs.nist.gov/nistpubs/SpecialPublications/NIST.SP.800-61r2.pdf, August 2012.

Incident Response Definitions

Properly applying the definition of an incident creates early success during responses. Cybersecurity teams analyze numerous situations daily. Clear definitions and subsequent actions keep informational and low-level issues at the analyst level and more significant issues in front of cybersecurity leaders. NIST (SP) 800-61 utilizes the terms events, adverse events, and incidents, as shown in Figure 3-1.

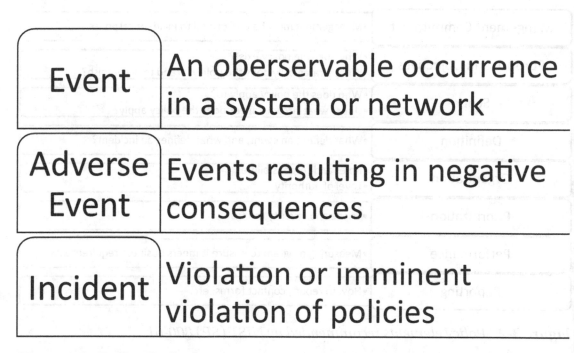

Figure 3-1. *Defined cybersecurity occurrences addressed within NIST (SP) 800-61*

An example of an event is quarantined e-mail that appears to be suspicious. A security analyst assesses the e-mail and decides either to release it to the recipient or eradicate it. System outages, whether malicious or accidental, fall into the adverse event bucket. Insider threats that remove data without authorization trigger a full-fledged incident response.

Policy Elements

Cybersecurity policy anchors all programs, including incident response, within the entity. Without policy, no mandate exists for the actions required to respond and recover from incidents. Effective incident response policies require specific elements, which are called out in NIST (SP) 800-61 and shown in Figure 3-2.

Mangement Commitment	•Management must be committed to incident response.
Purpose and Objectives	•Why does the policy exist? •What strategically does the policy intend to accompish?
Scope	•Who does the policy apply to? •Under what circumstances does the policy apply?
Definition	•What defines an event, and what defines an incident?
Organization	•Roles and responsibilities •Level of authority
Prioritization	•Triage and severity ratings
Performance	•Measuring program to ensure it meets business requirements
Reporting	•How to report, contact forms, etc.

Figure 3-2. *Policy elements recommended by NIST (SP) 800-61*

Statement of management commitment: Simply put, the policy states that management is establishing an incident response plan.

Purpose and objectives of the policy: This states the purpose of the policy: to establish an incident response program.

Scope and objectives: The policy must specify who it applies to and the expectations. It is feasible for the policy to dictate a reference to the incident response plan for this information.

Definition of events and incidents: The policy must identify what an event is, what an incident is, and how the responses to each differ. Just like the scope and objective elements, the policy can dictate that readers refer to definitions in the incident response plan.

Prioritizing or severity ratings: This establishes thresholds for categorizing events and incidents, based on severity. Again, to keep policies clean and avoid constant changes and approvals by the cybersecurity committee or management, dictate a reference to the plan.

Performance measures: Stating the identification and adherence to performance measures adds accountability to the program.

Reporting and contact form: Expectations for reporting via proper channels ensures no delays responding to issues requiring investigation.

To avoid cluttering the cybersecurity or information security policy document with procedure-type statements, policies dictate where individuals can reference more detailed information but still establish authority for the incident response program.

Plan Elements

Once the policy document is created and approved by management, incident response plan development begins. The plan acts as a blueprint for the incident response program. It outlines how to handle all events of concern from beginning to end.

The Team

The incident response plan identifies the individuals who make up the incident response team and their roles. Someone must own the plan. Usually, someone from cybersecurity, at the manager or director level, owns incident response. This is not a steadfast rule, if the owner possesses the necessary competencies. Supporting roles are also assigned. The primary response, also referred to as first responders, begins investigations when the plan is invoked. This occurs after the security desk or IT help desk escalates issues to the program owner. If the chief information officer (CIO) or chief information security officer (CISO) is not part of the initial response, he or she is brought into the response as part of a broader group. This is the point at which non technical members of management take an active role in incident response. Figure 3-3 shows the typical makeup of the incident response teams.

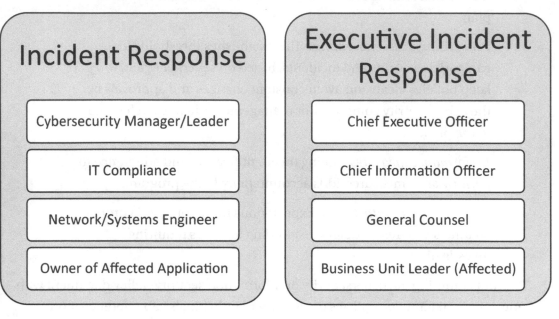

Figure 3-3. *Examples of incident response teams and key members of each*

Incident response teams are different across all organizations, and the preceding example is not meant as an absolute picture of how teams should be constructed. Larger organizations might need several versions of the initial response team, based on factors including geography, technology, or other reasons. Again, a larger entity might want an intermediate response team involved, before C-Suite executives are brought to the table. The CIO and other director-level associates are often the intermediaries between the response team on the front lines and top-level executives.

Mission

Success requires creating a program mission for incident response. Simple, purposeful mission statements give purpose and guide the team through incident response. Examples of mission statements derived from the cybersecurity mission include the following:

- Effectively identify, contain, eradicate, and recover from events designed to harm our patients and disrupt our business

- Keep our data, customers, and employees safe from cyber threats

A mission statement is unique to the team and leader of the incident response program, and the mission is built into the response plan.

Goals and Strategy

Jim Collins, in his book *Good to Great*, introduced the world to the Hedgehog Concept. One significant component of the Hedgehog Concept is to first decide who is on the team, then construct the strategy and goals. Many approach building programs the opposite way, but that does not consider the strengths and skill gaps of the team.

Many entities, not just small ones, cannot afford resources specializing in threat hunting or forensics, such as memory analysis. So, constructing the team requires a mix of internal members and managed service organizations acting as extensions of the internal team. Figure 3-4 displays such a mix.

Internal Security Team	Managed Security Service Provider Roles	Forensic Service Roles
• CISO • Security Engineers • Security Analysts	• Log and Event Correlation • Alerting • Threat Hunting and Analysis	• Log Review • Computer Forensics • Contain, Eradicate, and Recover

Figure 3-4. A cybersecurity program built on internal and external resources. The Internal Security Team box shows the makeup of a sample team, and the Managed Security Service Provider Roles and Forensic Service Roles boxes illustrate the roles those entities play in the cybersecurity program.

In the case of a healthcare entity, the goal of the program might focus on detecting, containing, and eradicating incidents before any healthcare records are breached. Events detected by the internal team or managed security service provider (MSSP) follow the same strategy designed to meet program goals. The strategy to detect, contain, eradicate, and recover from an event or incident at such a healthcare entity might look like the following, after initial detection:

- Gather all relevant logs.

- Direct the MSSP to analyze all systems for indicators of the compromise, to document all affected systems.

- Engage the forensic firm to review all logs collected for analysis conclusion, event severity, and next steps.

- If escalated, engage the forensic firm to contain and eradicate the intrusion and assist in recovering the affected systems.

The strategy here is to quickly and efficiently analyze evidence and gather as much data as possible. If the data suggests more than a simple event occurred, the forensic partner takes over the analysis, either advising escalation of the response or mitigation of the issue and closing of the incident.

Senior Management Approval

The backing of senior management is important. During incident response, the first responders make decisions, including taking systems offline, calling in forensic teams, and any number of other decisions affecting business as usual. Desired results cannot be achieved if the team is concerned about second-guessing during an incident.

Handling Internal and External Communication

Mistakes in communication can cause severe issues when responding to incidents. When to tell internal teams and when to notify external stakeholders affected by an incident is a matter requiring careful consideration. If news of an incident is leaked before all the facts are gathered, unnecessary damage can result. Conversely, waiting too long to communicate erodes confidence and integrity in the organization.

Road Map for Maturing the Process

Creating a road map for maturing the process requires measurement criteria. Understanding the program's current state remains a prerequisite for expressing the desired future state. There are several ways to measure the maturity of cybersecurity processes, a popular method being Program Review for Information Security Management Assistance (PRISMA).[3] Others include the Capability Maturity Model (CMM). PRISMA is a method to assess the entire program, including strategy, budget, and training. Alternatively, entities can focus on assessing program elements listed here:

- Policies

- Procedures

- Implemented and operating

- Testing

- Management review

Policies and procedures are the starting point. Without a policy that establishes the program, no authority backs the program to do what is necessary to respond to incidents. The procedures are the tactics used to respond to events. The who, what, where, when, and how is documented. As details emerge, more detailed tactics, contained in incident response playbooks, are invoked, based on the specific events encountered.

Implementation measures how well the process operates. Deviations must be documented and remediated.

Testing requires the use of metrics, which are measured per incident and over a period. Based on performance against these metrics, management review and recommended changes remain the capstone to a fully mature program.

Metrics Used to Measure the Incident Response Capability

Unless there is something to measure, it is impossible to know how well the program is performing. The challenge is developing effective measures. Table 3-1 disuses several common measures.

---

[3]Pauline Bowen and Richard Kissel, "Program Review for Information Security Management Assistance (PRISMA)," National Institute of Standards and Technology, 2007.

Table 3-1. Example of Metrics Used to Measure the Incident Response Program

Metric	Measurement
Number of Events	Events detected and investigated during measurement period
Number of Incidents	Events classified as incidents and investigated during the given period
Event/Incident Type	Classify events to understand trends, changes in vectors, or improvements in detection
Mean Time to Detect	When did the event begin and when did cybersecurity capabilities detect its presence?
Mean Time to Respond	Time elapsed between detection and response
Mean Time to Recover	Time elapsed between response time and eradication/recovery

Tracking the number of events and incidents is valuable for several reasons. Knowing that there is an upward trend in alerts increases the need for cybersecurity vigilance. Event and incident types can change over time. When new capabilities are added to the environment, it is reasonable to expect that event detection increases. Alert types may change too. An example would be the implementation of data loss prevention (DLP) capabilities. If DLP is new to the environment, an increase in detection of sensitive data in motion, in use, and at rest outside policy guidelines is possible. The mean time to detect, mean time to respond, and mean time to recover measure the time it takes to meet these milestones during incident and event response.

Procedure Elements

The procedure elements of incident response consist of the tactical playbooks, specific to attack types, that outline the steps taken to identify, contain, eradicate, and recover from these attacks. Basically, this includes everything required to report, respond to, and close event and incident tickets. Examples of procedural playbooks that must be available to the team include

- Phishing attack

- Malware/ransomware outbreak

- Inappropriate use of assets

- Data theft

- Unauthorized access

- Elevation of privileges

- Stolen assets

This is not an exhaustive list, but it covers very common scenarios faced by entities.

Sharing Information with Outside Parties

Incidents require communications with outsiders. Stakeholders possibly affected by the incident, law enforcement, and media want updates. The organization also needs to share information with third parties engaged to execute forensic investigation. Audit logs, memory dumps, and other artifacts likely contain sensitive data.

The Media

Documenting media interaction requirements in a document and providing training to individuals expected to interact with the media highlight preplanning activities. Attempting this during an incident triggers adverse situations, damaging public perception of the response. Those designated as spokespersons must be limited.

Law Enforcement

A strategic decision, which is made during plan development, is whether the focus of the response team is catching and prosecuting attackers or the resumption of business. If prosecution is an objective, contacting law enforcement is an action taken early in the response process.

Incident Response Team Structure

NIST 800-61 identifies three types of models for building the incident response team. These team models are a central incident response team, distributed incident response team, or a coordinating team.

Choices exist for staffing these models. Staffing strictly with internal employees, outsourcing the function, or a hybrid approach in which certain capabilities are outsourced depends on needs and available resources.

Team Models

Several choices exist for incident response team models, each listed here is available for organizations to use, based on fit and resources available.

- *Central Incident Response Team*: One team handling all incidents and utilized in smaller organizations.

- *Distributed Incident Response Team*: Multiple response teams. Used in large entities and broken up based on geographies or business units.

- *Coordinating Team*: This team coordinates or manages the response team. NIST defines this as a CSIRT for the CSIRT.

Staffing incident response with internal employees, partial outsourcing, or fully outsourced are viable options for filling in the team model chosen.

Team Model Selection

When selecting appropriate structure and staffing models for an incident response team, organizations should consider the following factors:

- *The need for 24/7 availability*: Is there a need for an around-the-clock response? Most organizations require this availability. It is also important to consider whether incident responders have to be on-site to respond effectively.

- *Full-time vs. part-time team members*: Most entities do not have full-time employees dedicated to incident response. The response team is usually staffed by members who hold other responsibilities. The idea is that, if an incident occurs, an all hands-on-deck approach is undertaken.

- *Employee morale*: Incidents monopolize time, and the responsibilities of everyone's day jobs do not go away. Significant incidents can require around-the-clock attention, eating into weekends and limiting time off.

- *Cost*: A dedicated team is costly in terms of adding full-time equivalents dedicated only to investigation events and incidents.

- *Staff expertise*: Who within the entity can add value to the team and assist in meeting the goals and expectations of the incident response program?

When considering outsourcing, organizations should keep the following issues in mind:

- *Current and future quality of work*: Is the outsourced entity providing value not available internally?

- *Division of responsibilities*: Who leads the response, the third party or the entity itself? Does the third party have authority to make decisions or take actions without the approval of the organization? These are key considerations when partnering with an outside firm.

- *Sensitive information revealed to the contractor*: This makes sense at government agencies, in which outside responders' access to data must be limited. The same is true for private-sector organizations. This needs strong consideration during planning for incident response.

- *Lack of organization-specific knowledge*: Does a challenge exist regarding knowledge transfer that can delay response time? Documentation including network diagrams and other artifacts outlining the IT systems and infrastructure should be readily available to the outside response firm. Many MSSPs offer incident response services. These entities might be good choices for response partners, because knowledge of the organization and IT environment should be present.

- *Lack of correlation*: This applies to detection of events. If a third party is engaged to monitor part of the entity and attempts to correlate events to uncover events and incidents, then the third party must have access to all logging sources available, or something could be missed.

- *Handling incidents at multiple locations*: Consider where the outsourcer is located, how quickly it can have an incident response team at any facility, and how much this will cost.

- *Maintaining incident response skills in-house*: Organizations that completely outsource incident response should strive to maintain basic incident response skills in-house. It is too costly to have the outsourcer respond to every event, and most agreements allow 24 to 36 hours before a team can be expected on-site. This time is critical, and it is an advantage if in-house team members can be working to resolve the situation in the meantime.

Incident Response Personnel

An incident response team requires a mix of personnel across the entity. Cybersecurity and compliance are obvious needs for the team. Infrastructure, applications, those affected by the event, and facilities are also needed.

Dependencies Within Organizations

It is important to identify other groups inside the organization needed to participate in incident response. This entails supplementing the incident response team with knowledge about the entity, its processes, and customers unknown to the response team.

- *Management*: Management owns incident response. It funds, allocates resources, and controls policy decisions.

- *IT support*: Not everyone in IT will respond to incidents. Unique events call for others to participate, based on expertise.

- *Legal department*: The general counsel's presence on the extended team or executive response team is expected. Engaging the legal department earlier should be expected in certain situations.

- *Risk management*: There will be issues involving cyber insurance and the management of risk that must be addressed at the corporate level.

- *Public affairs and media relations*: Large breaches garner media attention, and involvement of personal information requires disclosure.

- *Human resources*: This group's input becomes necessary when employee involvement is suspected.

- *Business continuity planning*: Systems taken offline because of the attack or when responding cause business operations to cease. In such cases, engage the business continuity team.

- *Physical security and facilities management*: Where facilities are outside the control of the entity, eliciting the aid of building management occurs.

Incident Response Team Services

NIST (SP) 800-61 discusses several domains. Incident response members potentially provide expertise and solutions for the organization. These include

- *Intrusion detection*: Discussed extensively in Chapter 2, incident response falls under the purview of cybersecurity team members at many companies and government agencies. Implementing Protect and Detect Function capabilities is an important task.

- *Advisory distribution*: Examples of advisory distribution include notifying employees of threats present in certain destinations, whether related to cybersecurity or personal safety.

- *Education and awareness*: Making end users aware of active threats and delivering guidance through newsletters, e-mail, and other mass communications increases the ability of this group to act as a first line of defense. More powerful communications consist of threats and concerns targeted at home computing and keeping family members safe online. End users' actions at home tend to be in line with actions at work.

- *Information sharing*: Management of intelligence sharing with groups outside the entity is facilitated by incident response. This includes groups such as an Information Sharing and Analysis Center (ISAC) or industry-specific groups.

Handling an Incident

Incident handling begins with preparation. It does not take a genius to understand that the time to figure out how to handle an incident is not while one is occurring. Detection does not focus simply on the technical mechanisms that generate alerts. It goes further, steering the team to think through attack vectors, precursors of an incident, and the use cases for notification and prioritization of events. This preparation accelerates the incident response team's ability to attain successful containment, eradication, and recovery of detected events.

Preparation: Preventing and Preparing to Handle Incidents

Preparation requirements inside NIST (SP) 800-61 establish this activity as a criterion for success. Preparation entails two steps: documenting attack vectors and precursors to incidents, as shown in Figure 3-5.

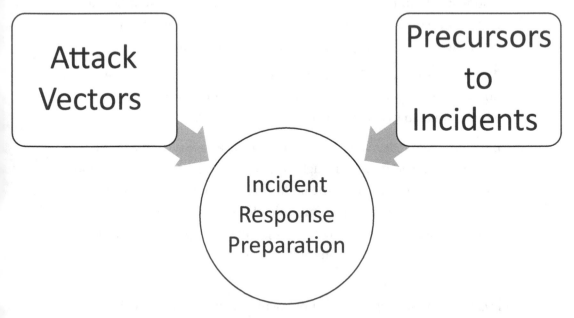

Figure 3-5. *Documenting potential attack vectors and the precursors to incidents are elements of incident response preparation*

Attack Vectors

How can attackers infiltrate the network and breach the confidentiality, integrity, and availability of data? Those attack vectors recorded during cyber risk assessments provide the clues. Vulnerabilities available when threats occur make up the precursors to events and incidents.

Detection and Analysis

Events and incidents are detected internally, or notification comes from third parties. Either way, incident response must act quickly, analyzing information and determining next steps. Many alerts are quickly mitigated and closed, and those do not require serious attention.

Containment, Eradication, and Recovery

Events not isolated to a single user or end point mean containment, eradication, and recovery procedures are executed. Data loss prevention, end point detection and response, packet capture, and log aggregation and correlation tools are used to search for the indicators of compromise (IOCs) on other end points. All affected devices must be detected, so that malicious artifacts are removed entirely from the network.

Post-Incident Activity

After each event or incident, the team involved in the response reviews the actions taken to understand if each was appropriate and what improvements are possible. Often, what is expected does not occur. This is true of the event and incident characteristics and of the response by the team. That is why post-incident response is important. Teams discuss what went well, what needs improvement, and changes needed. The goal is to continuously improve the program.

NIST CSF Implementations[4]

When building a cybersecurity program using the NIST CSF, the elements NIST (SP) 800-61 recommends are incorporated into the categories and subcategories addressing incident response. Those elements are useful for assessing the program periodically, to confirm each is still present. Details of the NIST CSF are located in Appendix A.

---

[4]NIST, "Cybersecurity Framework," www.nist.gov/cyberframework, 2018.

Detection

Detection capabilities are the front line of incident response. Detecting unusual and unauthorized behavior as quickly as possible is the first step in successful response. For that, certain technological capabilities supported by people and processes are required. Intrusion detection and analysis expectations appeared in the preceding outline of NIST (SP) 800-61.

Anomalies and Events

Anomalies and events focuses the entity on detecting and acting on unusual behavior. The events are analyzed in the context of the assets targeted and impact to the organization. Table 3-2 illustrates the subcategories of the anomalies and events category.

Table 3-2. *Subcategories of Anomalies and Events Located Within the Detect Function*

NIST CSF Subcategory	Objective
DE.AE-1	A baseline of network operations and expected data flows for users and systems is established and managed.
DE.AE-2	Detected events are analyzed to understand attack targets and methods.
DE.AE-3	Event data are aggregated and correlated from multiple sources and sensors.
DE.AE-4	Impact of events is determined.
DE.AE-5	Incident alert thresholds are established.

Common solutions implemented include

- Data loss prevention

- End point detection and response

- Intrusion detection

- Packet capture

- Security incident and event management correlation logs collected from network devices and servers

The strategy for achieving this through the anomalies and events subcategory are outlined in Figure 3-6.

Figure 3-6. *Strategy for detecting events, based on objectives of the anomalies and events subcategory of the NIST CSF*

After understanding what is normal in the environment, the focus shifts to detecting events through correlation of data and quickly understanding the potential impact to organizational assets when anomalies are found. Based on the type of event and risk involved, executing predefined actions mitigates potential harm. These procedures are discussed in greater detail in Chapter 4.

Security Monitoring

A more appropriate name for this subcategory might be "continuous monitoring," because that is the objective here. Everyone and everything are monitored—the network, the users, the property, and end points. The goal is to detect events. Table 3-3 shows the subcategories of the security monitoring category.

Table 3-3. *Subcategories of the Security Monitoring Category Within the Detect Function*

NIST CSF Subcategory	Objective
DE.CM-1	The network is monitored to detect potential cybersecurity events.
DE.CM-2	The physical environment is monitored to detect potential cybersecurity events.
DE.CM-3	Personnel activity is monitored to detect potential cybersecurity events.
DE.CM-4	Malicious code is detected.

(continued)

Table 3-3. (*continued*)

NIST CSF Subcategory	Objective
DE.CM-5	Unauthorized mobile code is detected.
DE.CM-6	External service provider activity is monitored to detect potential cybersecurity events.
DE.CM-7	Monitoring for unauthorized personnel, connections, devices, and software is performed.
DE.CM-8	Vulnerability scans are performed.

What is the strategy for monitoring the environment? When resources are scarce, deployment becomes strategic.

Note   A quick note about resources. This does not refer only to budget dollars available to spend on technology or head count. Time is a key element. The need for entities to run lean requires individuals to wear many hats. Prioritizing focus on high-impact assets is important for optimizing team members' time.

This means focusing the monitoring resources: personal activity, network traffic, malicious downloads, and physical security toward assets processing sensitive data and users with direct access to that data. This is not to say that risk does not affect assets and users outside these high-impact areas, but risk-based approaches might dictate focusing primarily on those high-impact assets and users.

Detection Processes

The detection subcategory focuses on roles and accountability for detection. Testing and improving detection processes are important objectives of this category. Table 3-4 displays the subcategories of the detection category.

Table 3-4. *Data Protection Subcategories Located Within the Detect Function*

NIST CSF Subcategory	Objective
DE. DP-1	Roles and responsibilities for detection are well defined to ensure accountability.
DE. DP-2	Detection activities comply with all applicable requirements.
DE. DP-3	Detection processes are tested.
DE. DP-4	Event detection information is communicated to appropriate parties.
DE. DP-5	Detection processes are continuously improved.

The objectives of the detection process subcategory help entities implement roles and responsibilities, test the process, conduct post-mortem exercises aimed at improvement of the program, and ensure pertinent information is communicated to proper stakeholders.

Respond

The Respond Function directs entities toward effective communication, analysis and mitigation of events and incidents, and necessary improvements to the program through lessons learned.

Communication

Communications encompasses several key components.

- Defined roles and responsibilities

- Criteria and processes for reporting events

- Sharing information internally and externally with stakeholders related to the event

Table 3-5 shows the subcategories of the communications category.

Table 3-5. *Communications Subcategories Located Within the Recovery Function*

NIST CSF Subcategory	Objective
RS.CO-1	Personnel know their roles and order of operations when a response is needed.
RS.CO-2	Events are reported consistent with established criteria.
RS.CO-3	Information is shared consistent with response plans.
RS.CO-4	Coordination with stakeholders occurs consistent with response plans.
RS.CO-5	Voluntary information sharing occurs with external stakeholders to achieve broader cybersecurity situational awareness.

Communication failures exacerbate the challenges when responding to events and incidents. Team members not following the process and communicating details too early get in the way. Understanding when to engage stakeholders, what information to share, and how to share it is just as much art as it is science. Sharing information with others, industry groups, or partnership organizations adds power to response processes, but entities must balance what each is comfortable sharing with the benefits of collaboration

Analysis

Analysis starts with the alert. Mature entities, with updated risk assessments, understand where critical data is used and stored. When alerts concerning these data assets occur, appropriate actions based on the seriousness of the situation transpire. Table 3-6 shows the subcategories of the analysis category.

Table 3-6. *Analysis Subcategories Located Within the Respond Function*

NIST CSF Subcategory	Objective
RS.AN-1	Notifications from detection systems are investigated.
RS.AN-2	The impact of the incident is understood.
RS.AN-3	Forensics are performed.
RS.AN-4	Incidents are categorized consistent with response plans.

NIST (SP) 800-61 and NIST CSF outline requirements for acting on detective alerts, the need to understand what assets are in play when events are triggered, and conducting forensic investigations. The elements of this subcategory often require supplementation from outside experts.

Mitigation

Mitigation involves containing and eradicating the cause of any event or incident. This includes new vulnerabilities uncovered during the response process. Table 3-7 shows the subcategories for the mitigation category.

Table 3-7. Mitigation Subcategories Located Within the Detect Function

NIST CSF Subcategory	Objective
RS.MI-1	Incidents are contained.
RS.MI-2	Incidents are mitigated.
RS.MI-3	Newly identified vulnerabilities are mitigated or documented as accepted risks.

Mitigation activities are covered by the containment and eradication elements of NIST (SP) 800-61. When outbreaks or intrusions occur, it is important to surmise the assets affected quickly, then determine how to remove the intrusion. Doing this quickly and correctly is critical.

Improvement

True to the program approach, the improvement category aims to ensure that incident response becomes more effective and matures over time. It does this by guiding the team to conduct lessons learned after each event and update the strategy and tactical plans. Table 3-8 shows the subcategories of the improvement category.

Table 3-8. Improvement Subcategories of the Detect Function

NIST CSF Subcategory	Objective
RS.IM-1	Response plans incorporate lessons learned.
RS.IM-2	Response strategies are updated.

If every opportunity is not taken to practice the response plans and find opportunities for improvement, a significant opportunity to prepare the team to respond is missed.

Recover

The Recover Function focuses on the steps necessary to bring systems back online. It is made up of planning, improvement, and communication categories.

Recovery Planning

Table 3-9 shows the recovery planning subcategories, which determine whether a recovery plan is executed during or after an event.

Table 3-9. *Recovery Planning Subcategory of the Recover Function*

NIST CSF Subcategory	Objective
RC.RP-1	Recovery plan is executed during or after an even.t

Improvement

As with the improvement category in the Respond Function, expectations that the team will review actions during an incident and document opportunities for improvement exist. These improvement opportunities are expected to be incorporated into the plan going forward. Table 3-10 shows the subcategories of the improvement category.

Table 3-10. *Improvement Subcategories of the Improvement Function*

NIST CSF Subcategory	Objective
RC.IM-1	Recovery plans incorporate lessons learned.
RC.IM-2	Recovery strategies are updated.

Improvement appears again in this function, because disparate teams or functions might be involved here. If a cybersecurity event or incident causes systems to go offline, perhaps the business continuity plan is also invoked during the response process. In that case, the business continuity or disaster recovery process in the case of significant incidents also must undergo a review for improvement opportunities.

Communications

Communications under the Recovery Function focus on how to handle public relations related to potential damage caused by the incident. Table 3-11 displays the subcategories of the communications category.

Table 3-11. *Communications Subcategory of the Recovery Function*

NIST CSF Subcategory	Objective
RC.CO-1	Public relations are managed.
RC.CO-2	Reputation after an event is repaired.
RC.CO-3	Recovery activities are communicated to internal stakeholders and executives and management teams.

Incidents and breaches potentially require expertise to repair public perception and minimize damage to the business. Engaging outside experts as a course of action occurs in many organizations.

From Guidance to Program Implementation

How does all the information laid out so far disseminate into building an incident response program? Establishing the program requires a mandate, which comes in the form of a policy. This gives the incident response program the power to evaluate and respond to events. Procedures and control processes guide the team's actions. Management measures performance of the program and adjusts accordingly. The goal is integrating as much of the guidance listed in NIST (SP) 800-61 as possible into the following categories when measuring the maturity of the incident response program.

Policy

The first item discussed in NIST (SP) 800-61 is policy elements. Those elements shown in Figure 3-7 detail requirements of effective policies.

41

Mangement Commitment	•Management must be committed to incident response.
Purpose and Objectives	•Why does the policy exist? •What strategically does the policy intend to accomplish?
Scope	•Who does the policy apply to? •Under what circumstances does the policy apply?
Definition	•What defines an event, and what defines an incident?
Organization	•Roles and responsibilities •Level of authority
Prioritization	•Triage and severity ratings
Performance	•Measuring the program to ensure that it meets business requirements.
Reporting	•How to report, contact forms, etc.

Figure 3-7. *Effective policy elements as outlined by NIST (SP) 800-61*

A simple policy statement giving power to the incident response plan and program is all that is necessary.

> *An incident response plan shall be documented and maintained by the Director of Information Security, who is responsible for implementing the plan elements and ensuring each is carried out investigating events and incidents.*

Establishing governance via the policy leads to defining the other necessary elements outlined in Figure 3-3. The purpose, scope, definition, and organization of the incident response program create the team. Prioritizing events, performing against metrics, and reporting guide the team through the incident response process.

Procedures

Procedures are laid out in the incident response plan and tactical playbooks developed to address specific situations. Each is specific-based on the type of event and role on the team. Common playbooks include

- Phishing attack

- Malware/ransomware outbreak

- Data theft/exfiltration

- Unauthorized access

- Elevated privileges

Breaking down the phishing attack playbook, the objective, scope statement, and response procedures for reported phishing e-mails are found. A high-level view, displayed in Figure 3-8, shows these steps.

Figure 3-8. *High-level stages of activities found in incident response playbooks*

These high-level sample processes outline steps taken when responding to phishing e-mails. Documenting the reported phishing, searching for IOCs, and determining the extent of the affected systems make up the steps taken to contain the situation.

Control Processes Implemented

Incident response controls are designed to meet the subcategory objectives of the NIST CSF and should incorporate as much guidance from NIST (SP) 800-61 as possible. Figure 3-9 lists examples of cybersecurity and incident response controls expected, based on the NIST CSF.

Detect
- Networks and physical access points are monitored for anomalous activity.
- Event data is aggregated and analyzed against alert thresholds established, based on impact to organizational assets.
- Detction process are tested and continuously improved.

Respond
- Communication and coordination of event information and activities are established and executed during events and incidents.
- Alerts are categorized and investigated, based on potential impact.
- Responses are assessed for lessons learned and response plans, strategies, and tactics are updated.

Recover
- Recovery plans are documented and tested annually.
- Execution of recovery plans during incidents and tests require performance of lessons learned.

Figure 3-9. *Example of control processes aligned with the NIST CSF, designed to direct the incident response program to meet established compliance requirements*

Dozens of control processes are required to meet the NIST CSF's objectives in the Detect, Respond, and Recover Functions. This subset is meant to show the need to customize the objectives established by the NIST CSF into internal control processes.

Measurement

Management must decide how to measure the success of the program. Meaningful metrics, ones measuring behaviors required to successfully detect, contain, and eradicate incidents, drive the tactics used to meet the goals and objectives of the program. Examples of metrics used in incident response are

- Average time to detect
- Time/average time to respond
- Time/average time to contain
- Time/average time to eradicate

- Time/average time to recover

- Number of deviations from the incident response plan

- Number of incidents detected

Response controls often have expectations for when responses to events and incidents are initiated. The metrics centered on deviations noted during a response to an event or incident are also important to management. These items, once measured, should be communicated to management.

Management Actions

Metrics and data do no good if action is not taken. If the time to respond or deviations from the incident response plan are noted, then management must act. This may cause new owners for the control processes to be appointed, the incident response plan to be adjusted, or the expected response time adjusted. These decisions are up to management. The expectation is that management documents its rationale for making changes to governance documentation or processes.

Summary

An effective way to build or improve incident response is to be systematic. The program begins by adopting a framework or guidance as the foundation, building the program using the chosen guidance or framework, then implementing the processes and capabilities necessary to meet its objectives. Timely assessment of progress points out necessary adjustments and improvements.

Two examples of guidance produced to establish fundamental requirements of incident response are NIST (SP) 800-61, detailing the elements of incident response expected of government agencies, and the Cybersecurity Framework (CSF), issued by NIST. The second outlines key processes expected by entities that are part of the critical infrastructure to respond and recover from cybersecurity events and incidents. When using the NIST CSF, reviewing the components listed in NIST 800-61 to ensure that the program is as comprehensive as possible adds more value to the program. The CSF covers the spectrum from responding to alerts through recovery, guiding entities through the process of developing controls. NIST (SP) 800-61 aids in building the plan and team that execute the control processes established by the CSF. Specifically, NIST (SP) 800-61 covers the following:

- Defining event and incident criteria

- Policy elements

- Structuring the team

- Communications

- Maturing the program

Using the elements of NIST (SP) 800-61, entities can incorporate leading practices into the cybersecurity program, no matter the framework used.

CHAPTER 4

Leadership, Teams, and Culture

Successful cybersecurity programs are built by strong leaders, developing strong teams and a well-defined culture. Culture contributes to the team purpose and facilitates the behaviors the team exemplifies daily, causing it to succeed. Urban Meyer put it best in his book *Above the Line,* in which he states that leadership is the difference maker.[1] Cybersecurity programs and incident response teams need strong leadership. The challenges for these groups are many, and leaders guide teams through challenges.

Hiring the most talented and intelligent malware analysts and forensic experts does not guarantee success, nor does only having a great leader. Balancing the talent mix across the team maximizes potential. A leader does not require superior technical skills to lead a team. Understanding attacks and the responses team members propose limits missteps. Leaders who are curious, willing to listen and learn, increase the potential for success.

Because entities are judged by the ability to respond when newsworthy events occur, equipping team members with tools to succeed and strive for continuous improvement are required to address the challenges hiding just outside the security boundary.

Leadership Qualities

There are many well-written books, articles, and other resources that hope to teach interested readers the qualities necessary for leadership. Each touts the qualities displayed by well-known individuals, such as Jack Welch, who ran General Electric for

---

[1]Urban Meyer and Wayne Coffey, *Above the Line* (New York: Penguin Books, 2015).

two decades, and Herb Kelleher, creator of Southwest, one of the most successful airlines of the late 20th and 21st centuries. Traits found in many leaders include

- Passion
- Humility
- Listening
- Decisiveness
- Emotional intelligence

Passion

Passion is a prerequisite for leaders. Without it, success remains awfully difficult. Passion pushes you out of bed in the morning and sustains you through the tough times. Cybersecurity possesses no shortage of challenges. Managing budgets, teams, projects, and keeping up with the volume of new information is daunting. It takes several hours a week, outside of daily expectations, for anyone to keep up with the latest developments in his or her area of expertise. Keeping abreast of other cybersecurity disciplines and domains is nearly impossible. Leading a team prepared to successfully respond to events, incidents, and breaches requires a leader with passion. Leaders keep the team engaged through the program mission, daily activities, and a desire to get better every day. The topic of passion brings Jack Welch to mind. Jon Gruden, head coach of the Oakland Raiders, proudly displays his passion for the game of football, so much so, that the title of his autobiography is *Do You Love Football?!*.[2] The subtitle says it all: *Winning with Heart, Passion, & Not Much Sleep.*

The cybersecurity and incident response leader who embraces the opportunity to build programs and improve them naturally attracts those with the same attitudes and behaviors.

Humility

Good leaders understand that they do not know all the answers. Closing oneself off to advice is ineffective and leads to trouble. During an incident, the leader of the response team must understand his or her gaps or weaknesses and allow those with strengths in those areas to perform without hindrance during the response. Perhaps web application

---

[2]Jon Gruden, *Do You Love Football?!* (New York: HarperCollins, 2003).

security represents a significant knowledge gap. Recalling the nuance of every possible vulnerability and attack scenario is not necessarily a priority. This is understandable given all the responsibilities on a leader's desk. In small and medium-size entities, those in charge of cybersecurity and the incident response program tackle budgets, personnel issues, project management, and program oversight. Getting into the weeds of every cybersecurity nuance is not always feasible. It is a balancing act.

Humility also means that program success results from group contributions and not because of any one person, especially the leader. When leaders want to take credit for success, it erodes morale and leaves the team deflated. Rarely is the leader the only individual with the right idea. In her article "The Importance of Humility in Leadership," Cheryl Williamson pointed to four traits of leaders with humility.[3]

- *Be willing to get in the trenches*: The team needs to know the leader works for them and is willing to work with them. Nothing is below his or her pay grade.

- *Think like a leader, not a manager*: Team members leave one-on-one sessions with leaders feeling valued, empowered, and important.

- *Remove ego from the equation*: Make decisions best for the team and not yourself. This build trusts. Making choices benefiting only yourself erodes trust and the team's belief in the process.

- *Be the change*: The team looks to leaders to set the standard. When it comes to establishing a culture, leaders must set an example.

Consider the following scenario. A malware attack is successfully defended before impacting the business. The outbreak affected a dozen laptops, but containment and eradication minimized the effect to operations. It's not likely the leader detected the

---

[3]Cheryl Williamson, "The Importance of Humility in Leadership," *Forbes,* www.forbes.com/sites/forbescoachescouncil/2017/09/14/the-importance-of-humility-in-leadership/#178458a32253, September 14, 2017.

malware or triaged the event. Rather, the leader empowered and instilled a sense of belief in the team to follow a process, as follows:

- A security analyst, help desk analyst, or someone on the front lines is alerted via the end user or detection capabilities implemented.

- This person consults with other members of the team, a senior analyst, security engineer, or, if monitoring is outsourced, a member of that team and the decision is made to take the device offline for further analysis.

- At this point, the team may report the situation to the leader, with the recommendation that the team hunt down other affected end points and take them offline.

- Once the team is comfortable, and all the affected devices have been identified, the leader is consulted and approves eradication of the malware from the affected devices and the testing of each, prior to them going back online.

- During these events, the incident response leader likely briefed his or her superior on the situation through initial and periodic progress reports.

In this simplified scenario, the leader was not the hero and did not deserve all the credit. Everyone did his or her job, resulting in a successful outcome. The leader listened, supported the team, and lent a hand when needed.

Challenges with incident response are caused by leaders who think they have all the answers or refuse to listen and pass blame while taking credit.

Listening

Leaders listen, not just during a crisis, but every day. When the team has questions or concerns, it is not met with a leader nodding his or her head, eyes glued to a computer screen or phone. Listening is a vital skill that leaders must possess. While it is easy to hear someone, listening is another story. When leaders don't listen, a frustrated team constantly repeats, "We talked about this."

John Maxwell devotes a chapter to this concept in his book *Leadership Gold*.[4] His premise is that the best leaders are listeners. Five concepts Maxwell puts forth in his book are

- *Listeners connect*: This is a prerequisite for leading.

- *Listeners learn*: Each learns by listening to others.

- *Listeners avoid escalating problems and issues*: Demanding results at the expense of listening creates problems of greater consequence.

- *Listeners build trust*: Team members share ideas and feel engaged with leaders they trust.

- *Listeners build effective organizations*: All the positive effects of listening allow leaders to push teams to new heights.

Why is listening to the team every day important to incident response? Having frustrations boil over during an incident because the team feels it is repeating everything ever said to the leader concerning incident response in the middle of a crisis causes instant failure. Nothing is more frustrating than a leader interrogating his or her team and putting everyone on the defensive, especially when the issue at hand has already been discussed with the leader. This derails the team from the objectives at hand.

Decisiveness

Once the leader listens to input from the team, asks questions, and gathers the known facts, decisions cannot be half-hearted. If an action appears appropriate at the time, execute the action without hesitation. Attempting to gain consensus or seeking additional confirmation from the team displays a lack of confidence in the process. If a leader does not believe in his or her program and the team's ability to execute, effective response is not possible. Worse, if the response leader lacks confidence and decisiveness in front of the executives, any actions necessary to address an event are met with resistance and doubters when responses cause business disruptions. Why would executives allow operational disruptions, if the incident response leader appears to lack confidence in the process?

---

[4]John Maxwell, *Leadership Gold* (Nashville, TN: Thomas Nelson, 2008), 49–54.

Emotional Intelligence

Leaders require emotional intelligence. Without it, effectiveness diminishes, and the program cannot reach its full potential. TalentSmart,[5] one of the leaders in the study of emotional intelligence and its impact on success, emphasizes that even the most talented individual's success is limited when emotional intelligence is lacking. TalentSmart breaks down emotional intelligence into the following elements, shown in Figure 4-1.

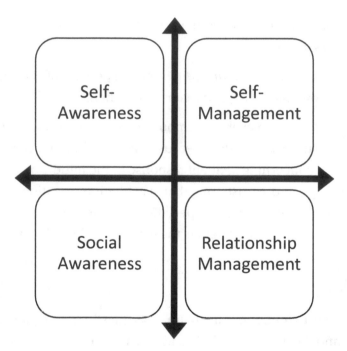

Figure 4-1. *The four skills of emotional intelligence outlined by TalentSmart*

Self-awareness and self-management make up what TalentSmart calls personal management. Social awareness and relationship management make up social competence.

Self-awareness means knowing how your actions and expression of emotions impact those around you. Displaying anger, frustration, cynicism, and pessimism affects your team and its performance. In their book *Emotional Intelligence 2.0*, Travis Bradberry

---

[5]TalentSmart, "About Emotional Intelligence," www.talentsmart.com/about/emotional-intelligence.php.

and Jean Greaves push readers to understand what triggers negative emotions. For this understanding to exist, one must continuously monitor him- or herself and the environment for scenarios and respond appropriately. This is self-management.[6] Incident response leaders require these qualities. If specific traits in others, or situations in an office, trigger negative responses, understanding this will be beneficial during an incident, and planning how to address such responses correctly keeps a leader from affecting the team negatively. For example, if excessive questions are a trigger, and a member of the team possesses this trait but is needed on the team, it's senseless for the leader to lose control of his or her emotions when the questions come. If the situation affects the response, the leader must appropriately move the process along.

Social awareness and relationship management refer to the ability of leaders to pick up on the emotions of others and use that information, along with knowledge of his or her emotions, to effectively work with others. Returning to the example in which certain team members ask excessive questions or what is perceived to be excessive questions, perhaps this person asks questions when stressed or unsure of his or her ability to execute. Understanding this, the leader must answer the team member's questions and foster belief in the ability to execute.

Culture

Culture is the atmosphere the leader builds. Ideally, it is one of connectedness to a purpose the entire team believes in and drives success. A cybersecurity program's purpose—relentlessly protecting an entity's information assets—is a purpose everyone can get behind. Results are driven by established behaviors connected to the program's purpose.

How They Build Culture at Ohio State

Urban Meyer created an effective framework for understanding how to instill culture in any team. These concepts are useful in instilling a culture geared toward cybersecurity and the incident response team. Figure 4-2 outlines how this framework fits into

---

[6]Travis Bradberry and Jean Greaves, *Emotional Intelligence 2.0* (San Diego, CA: TalentSmart, 2009).

cybersecurity and incident response. The behaviors expected of all members of the team include acting with purpose, intention, and skill.[7]

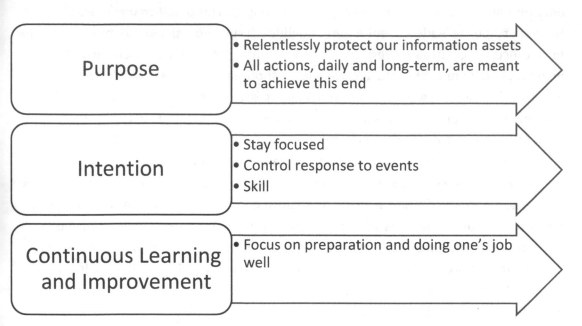

Figure 4-2. *Behaviors expected of members of the cybersecurity and incident response teams*

The behaviors outlined drive positive results. Each day, members of the team focus on protecting information assets, personally identifiable information (PII) of employees and customers, intellectual property, and financial data. The daily activities of the team center on this purpose. Anything not in line with this purpose must take a backseat.

Urban Meyer and Wayne Coffey write about the importance of controlling, or choosing, one's response to events. It's no secret that controlling the occurrence of cybersecurity events and incidents is not possible, and sometimes the outcomes of these events and incidents are not controllable, despite proper responses. Responding to cybersecurity events, however, can be controlled. Security teams and incident responders face this fact every day. End users circumvent controls, control owners choose not to operate controls, and senior management does not take security seriously. These are perhaps out of anyone's control. Getting angry, complaining, and giving up are poor responses. The team must accept the facts and do what it can.

---

[7]Meyer and Coffey,*Above the Line.*

Skills can be learned, practiced, and improved. Individuals and teams must strive for continuous improvement. Leaders are always seeking ways to improve leadership skills and technical skills. There are many free and paid opportunities to learn.

Improving Leadership Skills

Many opportunities exist to learn and improve leadership and other soft skills. Book learning is an old-school but valuable learning tool. In addition to those by Urban Meyer, John Maxwell wrote many books about leadership, success, and how leaders think that are worth reading. John Wooden,[8] the famous UCLA basketball coach, known for the school's prolific string of winning streaks and national titles, emphasizes preparation, teamwork, and effort as indicators of success. These characteristics are measured by wins and losses, not any scoreboard. Each of these leaders emphasizes that a strong desire for continuous learning resides within all great leaders. They never stop learning and trying to improve.

Institutions such as the Massachusetts Institute of Technology (MIT)[9] and Coursera[10] are two organizations offering learning opportunities. MIT's OpenCourseWare offering consists of courses taught at the university in the past. Several disciplines, including business, management, and leadership, are available. Coursera offers free and fee-based courses taught at universities around the globe. One can go to the web site and search for courses by topic.

Improving Technical Skills

As with soft skills, many opportunities exist to improve technical skills. Again, books are great. No shortage of books on cybersecurity and specific subjects, such as forensic investigation, malware analysis, penetration testing, and numerous others, exist. Electronic versions make it easy to carry several titles at a time to view during the day. Hard copies act as useful references for later dates. Either way, reading is an easy way to acquire desired skills and knowledge.

Sites such as Cybrary (`www.cybrary.it`) offer free courses in every domain of cybersecurity. Students can prepare for Network+, Security+, Cisco, and Microsoft

---

[8]John Wooden and Steve Jamison, *Wooden on Leadership: How to Create a Winning Organization* (New York: McGraw-Hill, 2006).

[9]MIT OpenCourseWare, `https://ocw.mit.edu/index.htm`.

[10]Coursera, `www.coursera.org`.

certifications, using free courses. Cybrary also offers courses on penetration testing, forensic analysis, malware analysis, web application penetration testing, post-exploitation hacking, and much more. It is possible to get a real education using the smartphone app.

The SANS Institute[11] is a nationally recognized provider of cybersecurity education. The instructors for these courses are at the top of their professions, and the knowledge gained through these courses will elevate one's career prospects.

Team Skills

To respond skillfully, the incident response team must practice. Too often, during tabletop exercises, members of this team are shuffling through the plan, trying make sure all steps are covered. This is bad enough, but if it occurs during an incident, disaster is imminent.

Note   Tabletop exercises are rehearsals. Scenarios are crafted, with more details presented to the team throughout the event. The purpose is to evaluate how the response team and executives handle the incident scenario.

With the amount of daily responsibilities cybersecurity and IT professionals manage, memorizing the incident response plan is not feasible. Practice sessions, as little at 15 minutes a week, can go a long way toward helping the team remember and recall steps in the plan. The team benefits by gaining a deeper understanding of the role each member plays during the response to an event or incident. Again, addressing these details during a live response is not desired. The result of practice is confidence and the ability to effectively respond.

---

[11]SANS, www.sans.org.

Alignment of the Team

Meyer called it 12 units strong—the idea that leaders must create cohesion within the team. In football, each position—quarterback, running backs, etc.—is coached by a leader. So are individual units, such as offense, defense, and special teams. The same holds for cybersecurity and incident response. Cybersecurity programs are broken into subprograms and owned by team members. Incident response is an individual unit and a significant part of the cybersecurity program. Smaller entities cannot appoint a single leader for each program. One person might have to lead multiple subprograms. No matter how the team is organized, all programs and all personnel must be aligned with the vision, mission, and objectives of the program. When members of the team want to take the program in a different direction and constantly oppose the direction of the program, cohesion erodes and losses occur.

Prepare to Handle Incidents

Success begins and ends with preparation. Incident response is no different. Assuming the incident response program is not established or in its infancy, there are several foundational items necessary to establish the process. These include crafting the strategy in the form of the incident response plan, creating tactical playbooks used to address specific incidents, and preparing the team through practice sessions and tabletop exercises.

Facilitating Organizational Change

As with building a cybersecurity program, the best way to initiate organizational change is to use a framework for guidance. Michael Kotter's eight-step change model and Kurt Lewin's change-management model are valuable references. Choosing either is a good beginning. Preference is based on the ability to implement. Kotter's model has more steps and considerations than Lewin's model. In the end, each drives change and improvements.

Kotter's Eight-Step Change Model[12]

The model developed by Kotter is designed to aid entities' efforts toward increased revenue or effectiveness. For incident response leaders, increasing the effectiveness of the program remains the outcome desired. Figure 4-3 shows the process in detail.

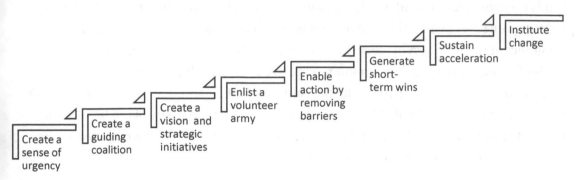

Figure 4-3. *Kotter's eight-step process for implementing change*

Figure 4-4 describes the objective of each step in the model and ways the incident response can use the model for specific objectives. Each step in this model lays the groundwork for the subsequent steps and the outcome the model is designed to generate.

---

[12]Kotter International, *8 Steps to Accelerate Change,* www.kotterinc.com/wp-content/uploads/background-photos/8-Steps-for-Accelerating-Change-eBook.pdf, 2017.

Create a Sense of Urgency	• This represents an opportunity for the organization. • Incident response can increase its ability to defend the entity.
Create a Guiding Coalition	• An effective group coming from the ranks is needed to drive the change. • If the IR leader is a manager or director, other managers or directors are needed to drive change.
Create a Vision and Strategic Initiatives	• Those initiatives, if acted on and executed, will make the vision a reality. • These are the key elements the IR leader needs to make the program more effective.
Enlist a Volunteer Army	• Large-scale change occurs when significant numbers mass under a common opportunity. • Gather as many from cybersecurity, IT, and other business units to aid in program improvement.
Enable Action by Removing Barriers	• This creates opportunities for employees to work across boundaries. • Including other business units gives clarity to the cybersecurity challenge and need for IR.
Generate Short-Term Wins	• Tracking and communicating wins energizes the team. • This can include new capabilities and improving processes and tactics. Whatever it is, celebrate it.
Sustain Acceleration	• Adapt quickly and determine what can be done every day to stay the course. • Practice breach response, Improve documents, and add capabilities daily, to increase effectiveness.
Institute Change	• Communicate the connection between new behaviors and entity success. • Tie the new processes and capabilities to IR's ability to protect from cyberattacks.

Figure 4-4. Kotter's eight-step change process applied to cybersecurity, information technology, and business teams

The change process Kotter proposes starts with the why. Communicating why change is necessary is another way to say change starts with creating a sense of urgency. Incident response is urgent. Attackers are constantly probing networks and searching for vulnerabilities. It is a numbers game. Entities must prepare for an intrusion. This is not meant to create fear, uncertainty, and doubt by suggesting that every entity will be breached. That may or may not be true; only time will tell. The sheer volume of e-mail sent to end users, and scanning conducted at the network perimeter, does increase the odds that something malicious can occur inside a network. This creates a sense of urgency. Incident response preparation becomes a must.

Being aware of this possibility, the incident response leader's job is to build a team of like-minded individuals ready to meet potential challenges. These individuals come from cybersecurity, IT, and other managers or directors from the business who are closely aligned to cybersecurity's objectives.

If the premise is that bad things will make it into the network, strategic objectives are defined to face those issues, as follows:

- Detect unusual activity quickly via technological capabilities and empower end users to detect and report unusual activity.

- Rapidly assess the situation. Can the security or help desk resolve the issue? Is escalation required? What assets are impacted by the situation?

- Identify all end points affected and contain the incident through the use of end point detection and response (EDR), NetFlow, stream headers and full packet capture, and other capabilities to capture the flow of data and communications internally and externally.

- Remove (eradicate) the intrusion from the network.

Investments necessary for these objectives require the leader to create the sense of urgency and vision behind the strategic objectives.

Kotter refers to the communication of this vision as "Building a volunteer army." Passion and excitement related to the potential for incident response's ability to defeat attacks by becoming a strength of the cybersecurity program is how leaders build an army of volunteers. No cybersecurity program has all the tools it needs. Funds are limited. Focusing on what resources are available and how each contributes to building a high impact incident response program instills realistic expectations in each volunteer.

Short-term wins are great for building momentum. Short-term thinking becomes a drawback when leaders forget to continuously remind the group of the long-term goals and create new short-term wins for each milestone. When building incident response from the ground up, completing the response plan and associated playbooks is a win to celebrate. Completing a tabletop exercise and remediating findings are other examples of short-term wins. There is a need to celebrate these milestones. Outside of incident response, when end users identify suspected phishing e-mails, communicating this success to the user base galvanizes the organization behind preventing these attacks.

Short-term wins are sometimes low-hanging fruit, meaning little effort is required to complete them, and very few challenges exist. To keep the team moving forward and prevent program initiatives from becoming stale, the leader must outline the daily or weekly actions designed to complete the initiatives. New or immature programs face challenges, such as the ability to globally reset all passwords. Certain types of attacks create this need, and if an entity has not thought through this process, it can implode on the team during a response. Automatically resetting user passwords through a PowerShell script, for example, might not be an issue. Service accounts are a different story. When those passwords change, automated processes and services might break. Some entities may not understand how many servers and jobs these service accounts are tied to. The last thing the response team needs is numerous alerts about processes crashing.

Institutionalizing change occurs when a business understands the value that incident response investment brings to the organization. Successfully containing suspicious events before impact to the business must be evangelized, to win the hearts and minds of end users and senior management.

Lewin's Change Management Model

Lewin's Change Management Model uses three distinct phases. These are Unfreeze, Change, and Freeze. Figure 4-5 shows these phases and the key pieces of each.

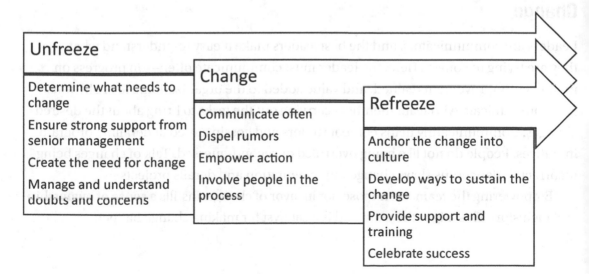

Figure 4-5. *Lewin's Change Management Model*

Unfreeze

During the Unfreeze stage, much of the legwork required to make the change process successful is executed. The incident response leader, desiring to undertake the transformation of incident response, should know the specific changes required. These change objectives range from additional funding, time to create necessary documentation and practice, and the need for forensic capabilities.

No matter what change is desired, sponsorship from senior management is necessary for success. The more support outside of IT the better. All the change items listed as desired changes, except, possibly, increasing the skills of incident response team members, must have resource commitments from management. But management must support incident response, by identifying its success as a key objective. Then the preparation time spent by the team is an expectation rather than a source of contention.

If gaps in the incident response program exist, the leader must communicate to senior management the need for changes and the dangers of not addressing them. This exercise is rarely successful when the risks are put into cybersecurity terms and not business terms. These risks are financial impacts and lost productivity.

Even with approval and support, doubts will surface, both with business leaders and inside IT, and even cybersecurity. The leader must address these and keep the process moving forward, so that the program can address events meant to cause harm to the entity.

Change

Leaders are communicators, and the best leaders make it easy to understand what they are trying to convey. Here, the leader must communicate often—on progress on initiatives, improvements gained, and value added to the organization. He or she must also communicate with team members carrying out the tasks to bring about the desired changes. Communicating helps combat rumors and gossip aimed at derailing program initiatives. People do not like being overruled or second-guessed. Talk of changes being incorrect or dangerous slows change implementation and derails projects.

Empowering the team, even those not in favor of change, instills a sense of ownership and inclusion. This aligns the team and is a catalyst for making change happen.

Refreeze

After change implementation, ingraining the change into the organization to avoid taking steps backward is important. Lewin refers to this as anchoring the change and developing ways to sustain the change. Since these changes are to a cybersecurity program, one would hope to ingrain the changes into the cybersecurity and incident response team easily. In Chapter 1, I discussed the cowboy mentality, whereby someone on the team wants to play the hero. Events detected by, or brought to, the cowboy's attention are communicated to other team members with a message such as that in Figure 4-6. Incident response leaders do not want to receive this message via e-mail, text, or whatever means is commonly used.

> I noticed unusual activity on production servers this morning. I took the servers offline and am scanning them for indicators of compromise. I think a developer downloaded something malicious, so I revoked his access.

Figure 4-6. *Example of communciation received by the incident response team when a member has taken action without sufficient discussion with the team*

The security desk, help desk, or analysts, depending on who represents the front line where events are triaged, is expected to follow the plan and either close an event or escalate. Problems exist when team members choose not to follow the plan. It is important that the process for incident response is strictly followed.

When changes are made, training is needed. Unsuccessful changes leave those affected feeling lost and frustrated. Unfortunately for most, this is more the norm than the exception. End users become frustrated when changes are made to processes—especially when technology causes disruptions to legacy processes—if communication, training, and support are absent. As the incident response team and program evolves, it is important for the leaders of this team to communicate why the changes are made and how end users can adopt new processes with minimal impact.

Finally, when changes are implemented, it is time to celebrate. Instituting change across the organization is challenging, and success must be acknowledged and applauded.

Summary

Whether the incident response program is unestablished or needs to mature to deal with adverse events, incidents, and breaches, there are several requirements. The first and most important is strong team leadership. Without it, success is limited. Leaders with passion, humility, listening skills, and emotional intelligence have greater potential for building successful programs. Change is likely necessary in the organization. Senior managers and members of the workforce generally are not equipped with an understanding of the tools needed to deal with cyber threats targeting the entity. Education early in the change process and painting a clear picture showing the seriousness of the situation creates a sense of urgency. Without it, organizational change is not sustainable. Models and frameworks designed by Michael Kotter and Kurt Lewin exist to aid incident response and cybersecurity teams attempting to implement needed change.

CHAPTER 5

The Incident Response Strategy

The incident response plan forms the blueprint and strategy for responding to events and incidents. It contains the purpose, scope, definitions and elements of incident response. Roles and responsibilities, definitions and escalation steps are common elements addressed in the incident response plan. The purpose presents the team with the "why" behind the plan. Why does the cybersecurity team care about planning for events and incidents? And why will time and money be invested in improving the entity's ability to successfully respond to incidents? The scope of the plan highlights the authorization given the incident response team to take necessary steps when dealing with events. Taking systems offline until confirmation that nothing malicious occurred will not be popular if business operations are interrupted. Roles and responsibilities dictate who is on the response team and how he or she is expected to act when events are investigated. Definitions are important as well. What is an event, incident or breach? Outlining these in the plan takes the guesswork and, it is hoped, the debate out of the process. This is particularly important when events are present. Debating these definitions in the early stages wastes precious time.

Purpose

Incident response plans are designed to protect the organization, maintaining the confidentiality, integrity, and availability of data and other assets, to avoid disruptions to business and reputational damage foremost. Data assets include intellectual property, trade secrets, strategy, company financials and customer information. These elements, if affected by an incident, could have varying degrees of impact on the entity. Purpose is why the incident response team exists.

65

Scope

The scope section establishes the jurisdiction for the incident response plan. Any anomalies affecting the assets and information systems of the entity will be investigated by the incident response team according to the plan. The scope section can contain roles and responsibilities of the leader(s). The leader of the incident response process is named here, and authorized actions are stated. These include calling together the initial response team, once an event is escalated, up to the leader of the team. Other examples include consulting legal, collecting affected devices, and consulting without outside forensic firms, if such firms have been retained and are available.

Scope sometimes outlines high-level overviews of the process, descriptions of how events are triaged, and the escalation path and steps for addressing events and incidents.

Definitions

This section clearly defines what constitutes cybersecurity events, incidents and breaches. Not all plans use these exact definitions. Some might use incident and breach; it depends on the entity. Events are normally any atypical occurrence in an IT system or network, that is, anything out of the ordinary that is detected. Mature entities with established baselines of network traffic and user behavior see more events then entities with less mature detection capabilities. An administrative login occurring during off hours is an example of an event. Normally, incidents are violations of policy and threats to the entity's assets. A user transmitting sensitive documents to third-hosting providers such as Dropbox in violation of company policy is an incident. Sometimes incidents become breaches. Breaches occur when unauthorized individuals view, change, or render assets unavailable. In healthcare, breaches are defined as the theft, misuse, or destruction of protected health information in electronic form, or ePHI (electronic protected health information). This would be confirmed via a risk of compromise assessment. In other sectors, breaches affect customer records, especially if those records contain personally identifiable information (PII), intellectual property, or trade secrets.

How to Respond to Incidents

Within the incident response plan, the strategy for the incident response program is outlined. This includes goals, roles, and responsibilities; how to analyze and triage events; and the requirements for escalation. The stages of the incident response and the strategies for each are also documented. The most common incident response phases are identification, containment, eradication and recovery. The strategic importance and objectives of each are outlined in these sections.

Incident Response Goals

The goals of incident response vary from entity to entity, but common ones include the following:

- Protect the organization's infrastructure, assets, and business operations.

- Comply with federal, state, and local regulations.

- Minimize the potential for negative publicity.

- Prevent or minimize financial liabilities.

- Minimize customer disruptions.

These are examples and may differ from entity to entity, based on the nuances of the business. What remains important is for management to work with the incident response and cybersecurity teams to document goals consistent with the needs of the entity.

Roles and Responsibilities

Roles and responsibilities state the expectations of each person on the team. Within the initial response team, the extended group involving legal, compliance, IT leadership, and external consultants, and the group involving senior management and external legal counsel, dozens of individuals have a role in incident response. No matter how the groups are organized and named, missing defined roles and responsibilities opens the door to chaos and actions not aligned with the incident response plan. Practice and discussion driving home better understanding of roles and the need to stick to actions outlined in each is important. It's not uncommon to spend considerable time during post-incident reviews going over roles and responsibilities, emphasizing the need to adhere to what's outlined in the plan.

Triage

When events are brought to the attention of help desk analysts, security analysts, or whoever is on the receiving end of alerts, it is up to these individuals to analyze and prioritize each. Many alerts are benign and closed by the analyst. Others require investigation before a conclusion is drawn. This requires escalation of the event. If managed security service providers (MSSPs), forensics investigations, and threat hunters are on retainer, conferring with these partners to assess the event might be necessary, based on the type of event.

Escalation

Potential incidents, by some definitions, are attacks against an entity's network that are under way. When incidents are confirmed, notifying the incident response leader commences and the incident response plan is invoked. The plan must include escalation of all types, when an incident is suspected. Internal and external legal teams must evaluate the situation, because business agreements likely contain provisions dictating breach notification time lines. Vendors doing business with healthcare organizations are required to comply with notification rules in business associate agreements. The incident response team must take the time to properly evaluate potential incidents, keeping in mind notification requirements, based on data affected.

Event and Response Phases

The response process is broken into several phases. Depending on how the plan is written, as few as three and as many as six phases may exist. Essentially, the phases consist of similar actions. These are shown as four phases in Figure 5-1.

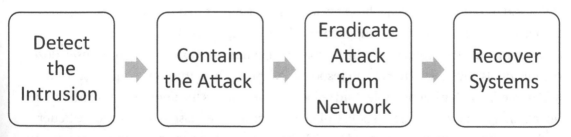

Figure 5-1. *Four response phases found in many incident response plans*

The first step is to detect events. How do entities strategically approach detection? They take a defensive in-depth approach and layer technical "tools" within information systems and the network, attaching operational processes and identifying the right people to own and operate these processes. Today, the detection strategy in many entities includes internal and external resources. Detection capabilities include numerous components.

- Intrusion detection at the perimeter

- E-mail gateways and spam blocking

- Data loss prevention

- End point detection and response (EDR)

- Log correlation and analysis

Effective log strategies require capturing logs from many different sources. Applications, servers, network devices and databases are needed to gain visibility over the entire entity. Outsourcing the correlation, analysis and maintenance of log capture and event correlation make economic sense for entities of all sizes. Successful partnerships are designed so that the service provider can analyze alerts and supplement each with context.

Containing the attack, identifying all the devices affected, calls for searching for indicators on end points and devices such as those present when the issues first began. With an MSSP or other service provider assisting, responsibility for finding all end points with IOCs might be better served with the service provider searching for other infected end points. The key is to compile a list of affected devices quickly while being thorough. The MSSP might achieve these objectives. Once identified, taking the devices offline keeps them from connecting or staying connected to others spreading the infection.

Eradicating the issues involves removing any malicious software and files loaded onto the affected systems. It also requires remediation, through patching or configuration changes, exploited vulnerabilities leading to the issues.

Once all the malicious files and programs are removed from affected end points and devices, systems are brought back onto the network, and production resumes. The cybersecurity team should keep a close eye on those systems, and the rest of the network, for signs the malicious software is present in the network.

Summary

The incident response strategy is outlined in the incident response plan. In it, the scope, definitions, and how to respond are outlined. The response section includes roles and responsibilities, how to triage and escalate events, and the steps to contain, eradicate, and recover from events, incidents, and breaches. All pieces of this plan are important, as each lays the foundation for tactics used to protect the entity from cyber events. The scope authorizes the incident response team to respond to events detected. Events are anomalous traffic and user behavior indicating that an attack against an entity's information systems may be under way. Incidents indicate a violation of policy and that intended damage to an organization's information assets is imminent. Finally, a breach means the confidentiality, integrity and availability of data assets have been compromised. This compromise is confirmed, and the incident response team must determine the extent of the damage, while executing the containment, eradication and recovery from the breach.

The incident response team, whether using internal resources or engaging outside firms with expertise, needs a strategy for containing and eradicating events and incidents. Many organizations use outside experts, because resource limitations make it difficult to employ individuals with expertise in these disciplines.

Roles and responsibilities outline expectations for each member of the response team. The importance of individuals following their activities in accordance with the plan cannot be overstated. When team members go off-script, trying to solve issues alone, problems occur. This is especially true when events are first discovered. Escalation requirements are also key. Determining right away the type of event—malware, ransomware, or other type of attack—and whether the malicious agent is a nation state, cybercriminal organization, or insider threat are factors considered when determining escalation requirements. The incident response plan's strategic guidelines are the blueprint for developing tactical measures to mitigate cyber events and incidents and avoid breaches. This document must be reviewed and updated by the cybersecurity steering committee each time events occur and annually.

CHAPTER 6

Cyber Risks and the Attack Life Cycle

Preparing to handle incidents requires thoughtful planning—planning beyond creating an incident response plan, playbooks and annual or semiannual testing. With limited time and resources, it makes sense to focus attention on areas in which cybersecurity events are likely to occur. Knowing where to focus is derived by answering the following questions:

- What risks invite attackers into the network?

- What attack vectors are likely to be used?

Two important tools designed to answer these questions are the cyber risk assessment and the Cyber Attack Life Cycle developed by Mandiant. The risk assessment lays out the risks present in the environment in which cyber events are likely to occur. The Cyber Attack Life Cycle outlines the process attackers follow when seeking to breach entities and steal, modify or destroy assets.

The cyber risk assessment and analysis entails several key items. Properly analyzing risks to the entity's digital assets requires assessing threats and vulnerabilities these threats are likely to exploit and analyzing each in terms of the likelihood of a successful attack and the impact to the entity.

Viewing these risks in terms of the Attack Life Cycle, formerly known as the Kill Chain, generates context in terms of an attack vector's threats. Think of it like laying the Attack Life Cycle on top of the risk assessment. A threat actor exploits a vulnerability to gain an initial foothold inside the entity. Then it searches for ways to exploit other systems, increasing its privileges, until the target is reached. Prioritizing the incident response plan and associated playbooks around these scenarios enhances planning and preparation for potential incidents.

© Eric C. Thompson 2018

Documenting Cyber Risks

Assessing cybersecurity risks requires six key activities. The first four are identifying assets, identifying threats, identifying vulnerabilities, and assessing the initial risk to digital assets in the entity. The fifth step is identifying security controls, sometimes referred to as measures, meant to reduce cyber risks. The sixth step measures residual risk, the risk remaining once a cybersecurity control is identified, and the effectiveness in reducing risk is measured. This is visualized in Figure 6-1.

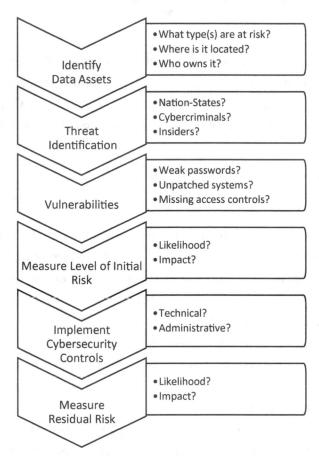

Figure 6-1. *The six activities necessary to measure cybersecurity risk*

Threat Analysis

Threats, both threat actors and threat scenarios, are people, groups, and events exploiting weaknesses in an organization's information systems, to carry out harmful acts. These acts target the confidentiality, integrity, and availability of digital assets. Figure 6-2 shows the three pillars of information or cybersecurity, sometimes referred to as the information security triad.

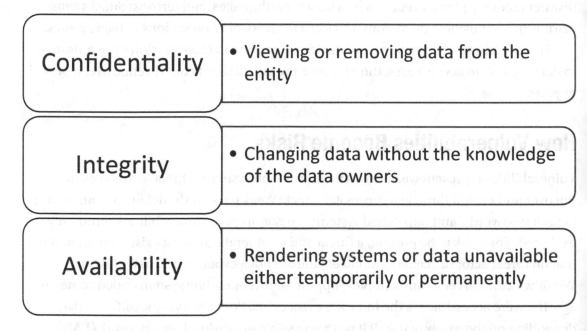

Figure 6-2. *The cybersecurity triad of confidentiality, integrity, and availability*

Cybersecurity attacks are targeted against one or more of the pillars shown in Figure 6-2. Attacks such as the Equifax breach target confidentiality of data. Data is viewed by unauthorized individuals, whether it remains at the entity or is removed. Attacks against data integrity result when a threat actor changes data without the data owners detecting these changes. Even when a breach is detected, these attacks are still problematic, because knowing what data changed is not always an easy task. Business operations are anchored in accurate data, so when integrity is compromised, business performance is impacted. Availability attacks include denial-of-service attacks designed to crash servers and other network devices. When networks are rendered unavailable, revenue and contractual obligations might be at risk. Ransomware is another type of availability attack. These are common and are reported in the news several times a year.

These attempts succeed when attackers successfully exploit end users who inadvertently launch malware designed to encrypt databases and other important repositories. Attackers expect victim entities to pay ransom to get the data unlocked. If the ransom is not paid, attackers threaten to destroy the data. It is important to know that backups with integrity exist and are ready for restoration purposes; otherwise, target organizations have limited options.

The last example of availability threats is included in business continuity and disaster recovery plans. Events such as floods, earthquakes, and terrorist attacks cause disruptions in business operations and force recovery of IT operations to backup sites.

Threat actors and scenarios cause incidents ranging in classification from nuisance to detrimental. In severe cases, threats cause the loss of significant revenue over a period of years.

How Vulnerabilities Become Risks

Vulnerabilities represent weaknesses in information systems. Threat actors seek to uncover and exploit these in a successful attack. Weak passwords, default accounts with default passwords, and unpatched systems are examples of vulnerabilities commonly exploited. For a risk to be present, a threat and a vulnerability must exist. Vulnerabilities that no threat actor or scenario would exploit are not a cybersecurity risk. Take a Windows 2003 server as an example. Support for this operating system ended some time ago. If it were accessible via the Internet, a risk exists. Possibly a very significant risk, depending on the assets at risk. If it were accessible on the local area network (LAN), a risk exists, but possibly a less significant one, based on the likelihood of an exploit. If this server is stored in a locked closet, with data not deemed valuable to the entity, and is not on the network, then, despite all the unpatched flaws in the operating system, no risk exists. Many confuse vulnerability scans with identifying risks. These "tools" place high and critical ratings on vulnerabilities found during scans, but these should not be thought of as risk ratings. A list generated by a Tenable or Qualys scan does not represent a list of risks, rather, a list of issues with context regarding the exploitability of the finding. Threat and impact context is required to measure the cybersecurity risk. Figure 6-3 shows this relationship.

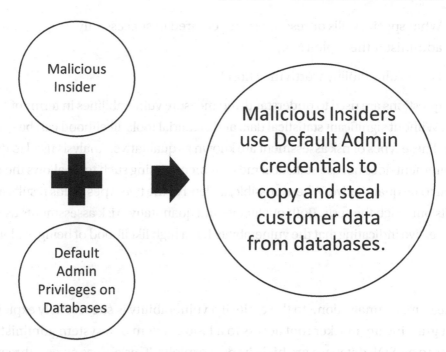

Figure 6-3. *A threat actor, in this case a malicious insider, exploits a vulnerability—default admin credentials—creating a risk to the confidentiality, integrity, or availability of customer data*

Once these relationships are identified and established, the seriousness of each risk is measured.

Measuring Risk Severity

Risk is measured using two parameters: likelihood the risk will be exploited and impact to the entity if exploited. Each has its own considerations for measurement.

Likelihood

Likelihood establishes the odds that a threat will exploit a vulnerability. This is based on several factors.

- How well known is the vulnerability publicly?

- What are the odds that the threat actors know about and can find the vulnerability in the organizations environment?

- What special skills or resources are required to successfully administer the exploit?

- Is the vulnerability worth the effort?

These questions are used to understand and measure vulnerabilities in terms of likelihood. Without significant statistical data and actuarial tools, likelihood can be subjective. These types of risk assessment are known as qualitative. Analysis used to develop risk measurement does not use statistical measurements. Using such tools allows the risk assessment to be quantitative. Where possible, a blend of the two types yields results in which the benefits outweigh the costs. Both qualitative and quantitative risk assessments use a scale of one to five, five indicating that the vulnerability has a high likelihood of being exploited.

Impact

Impact measures damage done to the entity if a vulnerability is successfully exploited. An exploit granting an attacker root access to a Linux system or a system administrator (SA) access to an SQL database are high-impact exploits. This access gives a threat actor the ability to do anything he or she chooses to the system and its data. Understanding impact is a function of several factors.

- The data the system processes

- The privileges exposed via the exploit

- Ability to detect the exploit or attacker's movements afterward

- Proximity to mission-critical data

The first three are self-explanatory. If the exploit in question exists at a health system, systems processing patient information are high-impact environments. Administrator accounts are high impact if attackers get access to them. Another consideration related to impact is detection. If an attacker gains access, allowing him or her to run PowerShell commands, for example, and detection tools are not present to detect its use, a high-impact situation might exist. The last item—proximity to mission critical data—considers where in the Cyber Attack Life Cycle the exploit landed the attacker. Does the attacker need only to find one more weakness to breach the target data? These characteristics are considered when assessing impact. Impact is also measured many times using a one-to-five scale, with five indicating the highest impact. Figure 6-4 shows a heat map, an example using the one-to-five scale for likelihood and impact ratings.

Risk Matrix					
Impact	Very High 5	Very Low	Low	Moderate	High	Very High
	High 4	Very Low	Low	Moderate	High	Very High
	Moderate 3	Very Low	Low	Moderate	Moderate	High
	Low 2	Very Low	Low	Low	Low	Moderate
	Very Low 1	Very Low	Very Low	Very Low	Low	Low
		Very Low 1	Low 2	Moderate 3	High 4	Very High 5
				Likelihood		

Figure 6-4. *Heat maps are used to measure risks by assigning values to the likelihood and impacts or risks identified*

Using the heat map, a risk with very high impact and very high likelihood is considered very high. Risks with very low ratings in both categories are considered very low. Every other combination of likelihood and impacts falls somewhere in between.

Review the Risk Assessment

Once the risk assessment is complete, the blueprint for planning and anticipating how a breach could occur is visually displayed. In Figure 6-5, an abbreviated example of a risk register produced during the assessment displays one high, medium, and low risk.

Ref.	Risk	Initial Risk Rating	Identified Controls (NIST CSF)
R01	Nation-States or cybercriminals could exploit servers, facing the Web or internally, moving laterally, with weaknesses owing to hardening standards/images not followed consistently.	Medium	PR-IP.1
R02	IT Ownership Assets are not managed correctly.	Low	ID.AM1 ID.AM 2
R03	Employees are susceptible to phishing attacks.	High	PR.AT.1

Figure 6-5. *A risk register showing high, medium, and low risk*

The high risk documented during the assessment states that employees are susceptible to phishing attacks. One way to reduce the risk level is to identify a cybersecurity control. To combat vulnerable end users being targeted by phishing attacks, a training and awareness control identified in the NIST CSF would be aligned to this risk. The amount of risk reduction, if any, depends on the maturity of the control process. Immature controls tend to operate ineffectively, and, therefore, fail to reduce the amount of risk. During incident response planning, the team would focus on preparing for attacks launched via e-mails directed at employees. Playbooks outlining necessary actions to combat phishing campaigns, malware, and ransomware attacks are key focus areas for practice sessions.

The medium risk illustrates vulnerabilities nation-states and cybercriminals can exploit in web applications. This one allows access to an entity's environment. The incident response team should plan for successful attacks against web servers and understand the relevant playbooks to contain an attack of this type.

The low risk shows that the entity does an effective job maintaining an inventory of hardware and software assets. The incident response team does not have to spend as much time planning for responses due to lost assets.

These three examples illustrate how the incident response team can think through scenarios in which events, incidents, and breaches initiate: critical and high risks first, then moderate as necessary, and, finally, low risks. It is probable that low risks are not part of the scenario planning and that only certain moderate/medium risks, depending on overlap with critical and high risks, are, for example, the medium risk owing to misconfigured web applications being exploited. If a high risk existed because out-of-date code libraries were in use, the configuration risk might be redundant and not necessary for incident planning purposes. The items on the risk register must be evaluated individually but should be considered where common attack vectors are present.

The Mandiant Cyber Attack Life Cycle

One important aspect of incident response preparation is game planning. Professional and amateur sports teams prepare for opponents before competitions. The purpose is to understand what the adversary does well, and what weaknesses might be exploited are key pieces of the puzzle. Mandiant's Cyber Attack Life Cycle, shown in Figure 6-6, illustrates the steps attackers take against entities.

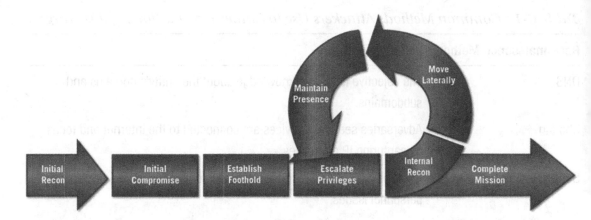

Figure 6-6. *The Mandiant Cyber Attack Life Cycle (formerly Kill Chain) shows the life cycle of attacks, which includes seven steps, from initial compromise to completing the mission. (Image courtesy of FireEye Inc.)*

Breaking Down the Life Cycle

The attack life cycle can be thought of as having three phases. The first begins with initial recon and ends once a foothold is established inside the targeted network. The second is an iterative process of escalating privileges, conducting internal reconnaissance, moving laterally, and maintaining persistence. The last phase is finishing the job.

Phase One

The attacks entities experience in today's environment are not quick hits, in many cases. This initial set of activities are designed to gather as much information about the target as possible. Attackers often know more about the network they plan to prey on than individuals working daily at the site of the targeted network.

Reconnaissance

Many methods exist for conducting reconnaissance. Open source tools exist for hackers to utilize, but much of the information gathered is publicly available. Table 6-1 shows common ways that attackers gather data to use against their targets and the benefits of this information.

Table 6-1. *Common Methods Attackers Use to Gather Information Against Targets*

Reconnaissance Method	Value Derived
DNS	The objective is to gain knowledge about the entity's domains and subdomains.
Shodan	Adversaries see what devices are connected to the Internet and focus on capturing IP addresses.
Social Media	Attackers can understand the entity, personnel, technology used, and personnel issues.
E-mail Harvesting	A list of targets at the entity can result in mass phishing campaigns that attempt to exploit an end user and gain entry.

Two common ways in which entities are compromised are through phishing attacks and exploiting misconfigured devices (more on this in the following section). Successful attacks are a result of extensive intelligence gathered before any active attack methods are launched.

Initial Compromise

If an attacker can trick end users into letting them into the environment, all the security controls at the perimeter and internally can be bypassed. Taking advantage of flawed configurations in devices exposed to the Internet is another way attackers attempt to infiltrate networks. Today's threat actors have the advantage of vast resources to take advantage of the intelligence gathered during the recon stage. If a phishing attack is the chosen method, attackers will know everything possible about the target, both personal and professional, to increase the chances of success.

Establishing a Foothold

Once inside, malicious software is used to establish a foothold in the environment. Successful phishing attacks lead to control over an end user device or stolen credentials. Exploiting web applications, for example, gives the adversary a level of privileged access that is useful. The objective requires placing a back door into the system, so the attackers can come and go.

Phase Two

This phase is iterative. First, privilege escalation requirements are met. These privileges are used to conduct recon of the internal environment and move laterally toward the objective, while maintaining persistence. When opportunities to further escalate privileges occur, or privileges to other environments present themselves, these credentials are used to execute internal reconnaissance again, keep moving through the network, and maintain persistence. This cycle continues until the mission is achieved.

Escalating Privileges

Once inside, the attackers want to escalate privileges, first by investigating the machine compromised, to see if any means of escalation exist. Cyber hygiene plays a role in limiting attackers' ability to escalate privileges. If default administrative or service accounts are pervasive in the environment, it is not hard for malicious groups to compromise one of these accounts to gain elevated privileges.

Internal Recon

Internal recon consists of investigating connections to the machine initially compromised and/or the machine currently in control of the attackers. Using Nmap to uncover connections is possible. It depends on whether the attacker thinks detection capabilities exist to alert the entity of the scanning.

Move Laterally

Once an attacker gets inside and maps a lay of the land, it is time to move around. The intent is to find credentials with the ability to get into systems housing the data targeted by the attacker. This includes gaining entry into machines that are literally lateral moves, meaning no elevation of credentials occurs, and finding machines in which elevated credentials exist.

Maintain Presence

Attacks are carried out over several months. Some statistics report a seven-month lag or more before detection of intrusions. This means threat actors come and go. They do this by implementing a back door, allowing access when time to continue the attack exists. One simple way is through the use of Telnet. Attackers also use rootkits. Rootkits modify system files, leaving back doors in systems as another means of maintaining persistence. If monitoring capabilities are immature, enabling this service makes reconnection easy.

Phase Three—Complete the Mission

This is a single-step phase. Once the attacker has found what he or she is looking for, removing changing, or destroying the data comes next. If the attacker wants to steal data, it is moved via irregular means and in small enough increments not to cause alarm.

How This Helps

Using the preceding, the incident response team develops threat scenarios. Accomplishing this requires thinking several key points through.

- The attackers targeting the entity

- The methods used to conduct the attack and complete the mission

- Weaknesses it exploits

- Similar weaknesses within the entity

- Actions available to reduce likelihood of success

Tie the Risk Assessment and Kill Chain

Two common ways in which attacks were launched in the last several years were via exploiting end users through phishing attacks and exploiting configuration weaknesses in web applications. These attack vectors represent ways attackers initially gain entry and establish a foothold in entities. These risks, if high or medium, require consistent monitoring and assessment. Measuring the level of risk for end-user vulnerability and securing web applications for changes keep the entity on its toes and focused on common ways events, incidents, and breaches begin.

Targeting End Users

Phishing attacks are used either to gain entry and establish a foothold for the attacker or to unleash ransomware. Beginning with the attack on Anthem, 2015 became a year of large breaches, owing to phishing attacks. These attacks targeted healthcare entities and captured many headlines. Anthem's attack began with a well-crafted spear phishing attack aimed at an individual with elevated credentials. The e-mail setting off the chain of events led the target to a malicious domain.

Targeting Web Applications

The Equifax breach reminded everyone how important basic configuration management and security of web applications is to entities. Equifax faced intense criticism because its breach began when a vulnerability did not get patched.

OWASP Top Ten

The Open Web Application Security Project (OWASP)[1] was established to develop and maintain secure applications. Every other year, the group publishes a top-ten list of security risks related to web applications. Figure 6-7 shows the version published in 2017.

A1: Injection

A2: Broken Authentication

A3: Sensitive Data Exposure

A4: XML External Entities

A5: Broken Access Control

A6: Security Misconfiguration

A7: Cross-Site Scripting

A8: Insecure Deserialization

A9: Using Components with Known Vulnerabilities

A10: Insufficient Logging and Monitoring

Figure 6-7. *OWASP top-ten security risks published in 2017*

---

[1]OWASP, "OWASP Top 10—2017," www.owasp.org/images/7/72/OWASP_Top_10-2017_%28en%29.pdf.pdf, 2017.

- *A1: Injection*: Common in SQL, NoSQL, and other platforms, this flaw allows for the execution of commands by these platforms causing data exposure to the attacker.

- *A2: Broken Authentication*: Insecure configurations of authentication mechanisms and session management lead to attackers capturing session tokens or passwords. Attackers can impersonate individuals using these credentials.

- *A3: Sensitive Data Exposure*: Web applications and APIs expose sensitive data when moving from web servers to the browser, if traveling in the clear.

- *A4: XML External Entities*: These attacks target XML-based web services by uploading or include hostile code in an XML document.

- *A5: Broken Access Control*: This issue occurs when entities do not configure authorizations for users correctly. Authenticated users who are not configured correctly allow users to interact with data not intended by the data owners.

- *A6: Security Misconfiguration*: There are many ways application misconfiguration can occur, making this a very common risk. The misconfigurations result from unchanged default settings to configuration changes not fully vetted for security issues.

- *A7: Cross-Site Scripting (XSS)*: Missing validation checks allow user input to update or end up in web pages.

- *A8: Insecure Deserialization*: Often difficult to execute, because available exploits require customization, these attacks occur when attackers substitute malicious data and rebuild it into a malicious object.

- *A9: Using Components with Known Vulnerabilities*: Libraries, frameworks, and modules with vulnerabilities are easily exploited. Entities not consistently testing for and remediating these vulnerabilities leave themselves exposed to exploits available in the wild.

- *A10: Insufficient Logging and Monitoring*: If web applications are not monitored for exploitation of vulnerabilities, attackers can use these to establish a foothold and pivot to other parts of the network.

These risk items are not unusually sophisticated. Threat actors know how to find these issues and exploit them without too much effort. If not already completed, it is important for the entity to test web applications for the presence of these issues. If any exist, the incident response team must plan for and anticipate cybersecurity events related to these events. How is this accomplished? By focusing detective capabilities and resources on these risks, if remediation is not possible or the team believes recurrence is possible. Regarding response playbooks, these would focus on compromised credentials, data theft, malware/ransomware outbreaks, or denial of service, depending on the exploit.

Summary

Planning responses to cybersecurity events is very similar to game planning in sports or military battle planning. Considering how adversaries attack based on their preferred methods and what weaknesses exist in the information systems focuses the team on specific actions to increase the effectiveness of the incident response program. Understanding what risks to assets exist is a must. Discussing these risks in terms of how sophisticated attackers approach targets helps the team build a comprehensive program aimed at preparing to handle events with the potential to occur.

CHAPTER 7

Detection and Identification of Events

Incident response begins with the detection and identification of events. Detection, a function found in the NIST Cybersecurity Framework, should be deployed based on risks identified and potential attack patterns of known threats. Many of the capabilities discussed in this chapter play roles in other elements of incident response. Several provide automated detection and identification. Automation is desirable when it lowers costs, increases efficiency and is more reliable than manual processes. A significant use case for automation exists when technology correlates and detects behavior patterns and activity not always seen easily with the human eye. Considering the vast amounts of data produced by entities these days, detection requires automated means to support information security and incident response teams. As nice as automation is, automating everything is not possible, and some form of manual controls must also exist.

Capabilities common in many entities' detection and response functions include

- Data loss prevention (DLP)

- Data capture, including NetFlow and full packets

- End point detection and response

- Intrusion detection systems (IDS)

- Firewalls

- Routers and switches

- Domain name system (DNS)

- Application and infrastructure monitoring

- Security incident and event management (SIEM)

Implementing these technologies requires care. Not defining use cases—specific scenarios in which risks and security gaps the solution is designed to detect exist—causes implementation gaps and mismanagement. These capabilities possibly alert the organization to an event or incident, or are used to confirm whether an event or incident took place and must be investigated.

Building Detective Capabilities

To detect events, basic capabilities, and technology, people who understand these are needed. These technologies require resources to tune and maintain the implementation, so that the right events are detected and nonevents don't waste resources with unnecessary investigations. The choice of whether to implement each comes down to financial and risk-based decisions. Implementing these types of capabilities takes time away from other priorities. The trick lies in balancing the choices, based on cost factors and gains in risk reduction.

Not all detection requires technology. End users are an example of how the human element can be very effective, such as noticing phishing e-mails first when other employees do not observe good e-mail hygiene.

Data Loss Protection

DLP is a necessary solution designed to detect sensitive data in motion, in use, and at rest. For example, if DLP is implemented at a healthcare organization, it is expected to address situations in which data is transmitted, stored and used in insecure ways. This might involve e-mailing patient data in clear text, storing it in SharePoint or OneDrive, printing it or saving it to a thumb drive. Many DLP solutions contain Health Insurance Accountability and Portability Act (HIPAA) rulesets out of the box. Other common out-of-the-box rules include financial, personally identifiable information (PII) and credit card data detection rules.

Implementing DLP

DLP implementation comes with challenges. Tuning the rules to reduce or avoid false positives takes time and effort. Creating an operational and repeatable process for dealing with detection alerts is required for the implementation to be effective. DLP can be set to alert only the cybersecurity team, to alert the end user and ask him or her to take some action prior to transmitting data and correct situations by blocking and encrypting. This process is driven by understanding what data is in the environment and the sensitivity of each type. One way to establish this is through a matrix establishing how data should be handled in certain states. Figure 7-1 illustrates data use cases.

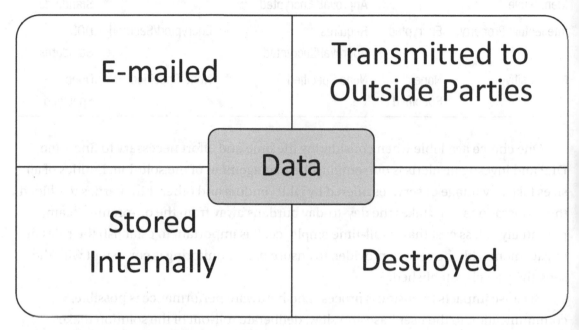

Figure 7-1. *Matrix showing examples of data states*

What makes the implementation and operation of this capability successful is applying the use cases in Figure 7-1 to actions required when specific data types are viewed from a security perspective. Table 7-1 shows the use cases and actions necessary for sample data types.

Table 7-1. *Matrix Outlining How Specific Data Types Must Be Handled for Given Scenarios When Detected by a DLP Solution*

Data Type	E-mailed	Transmitted to Outsiders	Stored Internally	Destroyed
Personally Identifiable	Encrypted	Requires Approval/ Encrypted	Encrypted/Secured	DOD Standards
Intellectual Property	Encrypted	Requires Approval/Encrypted	Encrypted/Secured	DOD Standards
Nonsensitive	None Specified	None Specified	None Specified	None Specified

One choice available when considering the time and effort necessary to fine-tune DLP and investigate alerts is outsourcing the management of the solution. Entities of all sizes take advantage of services offered by DLP vendors and other third parties to offload these operations. This takes the day-to-day burdens away from the on-premise team, potentially at less cost than a full-time employee. It is important to establish the rules of engagement with the service provider, to ensure data monitoring is consistent with the sensitivity levels established.

Because impacts to business process and hardware performance is possible, communication to the user base and slow, deliberate roll-out of the solution makes sense. The last thing the information security team needs is an implementation resulting in a business slowdown.

Handling the Data Types

Data traverses the network and is transmitted to customers and business partners. DLP detects instances in which the data types in question are in motion. Sensitive data headed out of the organization, in clear text, is usually prohibited and must be prevented. Some data at rest requires storage in secure places. Allowing sensitive data to sit in SharePoint sites, One Drive, or, in some cases, on laptops, is usually a policy violation. DLP is used to identify instances in which data is stored in violation of policy. Again, the solution can simply alert, encrypt the data where it is located or move the data and leave behind a note with the new location where the data is at rest. The actions of encrypting or moving usually occur after the solution has been in place for a while and the likelihood of a false positive is lower.

End Point Detection and Response

End point detection and response is a capability used to detect changes made to end points consistent with known indicators of attack or behavior and inconsistent baselines of normal behavior. This is done by recording what takes place in an end point—configuration, file, and user accounts—and storing it for review and analysis when necessary. Entities can store this data in a database or aggregate it with other data and logs in a correlation solution like SIEM. These solutions act in a front-line detection capacity and are valuable during containment. Some implementations utilize behavior analytics and machine intelligence to alert of possible security events. These solutions allow the team to quickly respond to the event and take appropriate action. Some common players in this space include

- FireEye Endpoint Security
- Carbon Black's Cb Response
- Cybereason Total Enterprise Protection
- Symantec Endpoint Protection
- CrowdStrike Falcon Insight

This is a short list of players in this space, and differentiating each takes time and research. A full list can be found on the Gartner Peer Insights review.[1]

Analyzing Traffic

Packet capture aids incident response teams' need to confirm whether suspected events exist. Organizations implement these solutions based on the incident response and monitoring strategy. Entities can choose to capture full packets, headers, and stream headers (the header and a portion of the packet contents), depending on program needs and the solutions offerings. NetFlow is another option. Developed by Cisco, NetFlow allows entities to capture data on the origination, destination, and amount of traffic. According to Michael Patterson, in his blog, Plixer, discussing the difference between

---

[1]Gartner Peer Insights, www.gartner.com/reviews/market/endpoint-detection-and-response-solutions.

NetFlow and packet capture, information provided by NetFlow is improving.[2] Network devices enabled with NetFlow collect this data for review. On occasion, NetFlow information is necessary to identify where traffic is originating from in the network, to detect anomalous behavior. If DNS server activity spikes, NetFlow information captured coming into the DNS server informs analysts where traffic originated from inside the entity, so that the end point can be investigated further.

Capturing full packets is the ideal method to analyze traffic but is very costly. The volume of data storage is cost-prohibitive in both storage and maintenance. Full-packet capture requires strategic deployment and specific use cases. Therefore, NetFlow is an effective alternative during traffic analysis. This data can be used, not only for incident response, but infrastructure teams use it to troubleshoot performance issues. Most firewalls and routers on the market are capable of capturing NetFlow traffic.

There are many solutions to choose from when implementing this capability. The major network hardware manufacturers offer this capability, and niche players exist, adding threat intelligence on top of packet and NetFlow traffic analysis.

Security Incident and Event Management

The age of big data affects cybersecurity teams as much as it does information technology and business folks. Understanding what data is within reach and what answers are available is challenging. SIEM capabilities are a focal point of cybersecurity programs today. As a detection capability, SIEMs require quality input to provide valuable output. Implementing SIEM requires a strategy and design to address the nuances of the environment and what is at stake. This is done through the development of use cases, designed to address risks and attack vectors identified through planning. Figure 7-2 provides examples of some use cases entities can utilize.

---

[2]Michael Patterson, "NetFlow vs. Packet Capture," Plixer, `www.plixer.com/blog/general/netflow-vs-packet-capture`, September 22, 2016.

Detect Unauthorized Network Traffic	This use case focuses on detecting patterns indicating an attacker's presence in the network.
Detect Patterns in Malicious Traffic	Attackers may use several vectors during an attack. Correlating those patterns in the SIEM is necessary to detect attacks.
Correlate Attacks with Known Vulnerabilities	Consistent vulnerability scanning allows the security team to correlate attack vectors meant to exploit those vulnerabilities.
Malicious E-Mail Activity	Patterns indicating attackers are using e-mail in an attempt to access the network.
Detect Anomalous User Activity	Indications of abnormal system usage, abnormal use of credentials, or escalation of credentials.
Protect Critical Assets	Focus log correlation and detection around assets processing the most sensitive data.
Detect End Point Attacks	Focus on attacks designed to compromise end points. Often phishing e-mails and other attack vectors begin with a compromised laptop.
Detect Remote Access Attacks	Detect activities indicating misuse of remote access methods used by outsider and insider threats.

Figure 7-2. Examples of use cases that entities can use to correlate potential malicious activities

Once use cases are identified, determining what logs and information must be ingested into the SIEM is next. Over time, new use cases are identified, and feeding of the SIEM is updated. This is how the capability is matured.

Note   These are by no means the only use cases for using a SIEM solution. The examples shown are meant to teach readers how to build a SIEM process and fit it into the incident response process.

Entities can create use cases around detecting attacks against web assets, lateral movement, and other insider threat vectors. Over time, as the threats, vulnerabilities, and risks are better understood within the entity, new use cases are developed and monitored within the security operations center.

Empowering End Users

End users are a detection capability. E-mails directed at them intended to gain a foothold inside the entity land in in-boxes every day. When end users identify malicious e-mails, it prevents successful attacks and allows the security team to see the methods attackers are employing against them. How savvy the end users are determines how effective this group is at detecting attempts to infiltrate the network. One way to increase the effectiveness of the end users is through training with phishing simulations. These simulations must be done with the intent to partner with end users and not as a method to catch them doing something wrong and calling them out on it. The idea is to keep security and a cautiously suspicious eye on e-mail communication from unknown sources. It serves as another capability to detect events early.

Other Ways of Detecting and Identifying Events

Intrusion detection systems (IDS), firewalls, application and infrastructure logs, and database and operating systems are other sources of alerts and evidence used to confirm that an event or incident occurred.

Intrusion detection systems work at the network level, analyzing traffic traversing between hosts and at the host. These solutions are intended to identify unusual behavior and events known to be malicious. These solutions use known indicators and intelligence captured from past events by the solution provider, and advanced implementations use artificial intelligence or machine learning to understand what is normal inside a network and on a host. These devices can be stand-alone or come packaged within other solutions.

Firewalls are primarily a prevention capability, but traffic passing through it can be archived and used to correlate events. Discussed earlier in this chapter were NetFlow capabilities especially. The firewalls collect data related to all traffic coming into and out of the network and traffic blocked. This is important evidence when investigating all types of events.

Depending on the application, auditing features capture successful and unsuccessful login attempts, user activity and configuration changes. Not all applications offer this extensive logging, but if available, entities should utilize it.

Domain Name System (DNS) logs and cache capture connections to known malicious IP addresses and domains.

Routers and switches contain log data from traffic passing through used during investigations.

Infrastructure logs come from databases and operating systems. These logs capture events specific to the server's hosting applications and databases. The most commonly used operating systems are Windows and Linux/UNIX. Each type comes with the ability to audit certain events. Table 7-2 shows categories of events captured by Windows Event Logs identified by Microsoft.[3]

Table 7-2. *Events Captured by Windows Event Logs*

Windows Event Category	Description
Account Logon	Credential Validation
Account Management	Changes to computer, user and group accounts
Detailed Tracking	Encryption events, process creation, process termination and RPC events
DS Access	Active Directory access
Logon/Logoff	Successful logons and logoffs by user
Object Access	Access to files, folders, applications, and registry
Policy Change	Changes to audit policies
Privilege Use	Audit the use of privileges
System	Changes to security subsystem

Some of these categories can add further granularity to the event logging. System administrators can evaluate these options and discuss with the team. If possible, forwarding these event logs to a SIEM solution facilitates efficient and reliable event correlation. Attacks often cause seemingly unrelated events to occur in multiple devices.

Linux also captures specific events. Those are outlined in Table 7-3. These examples were recommended by Lenny Zeltser on his web site.[4]

---

[3]Orin Thomas, "Administering Windows Server 2012 R2: Monitoring and Auditing," www.microsoftpressstore.com/articles/article.aspx?p=2217266&seqNum=3, June 2, 2014.

[4]Lenny Zeltser, "Critical Log Review Checklist for Security Incidents," https://zeltser.com/security-incident-log-review-checklist/, June 18, 2016.

Table 7-3. *Events Captured by Linux Logging Capabilities*

Linux Event Logged
Successful User Login
Failed User Login
User Logoff
Changes to User Accounts or Deleted Accounts
Sudo Actions
Service Failures

Just as in the Windows scenario, the best use of the logs collected are via analysis by a SIEM or another log-correlation tool.

Depending on the database in use, some variance of events captured exists across the different types. Many database events of interest are like those mentioned in the Windows and Linux event logging: successful and failed login attempts, changes to accounts, changes to data structures and schemas and privileged actions. These events deliver clues to suspicious activity in these environments.

Identification of Security Events

Security events and incidents are detected in many ways. End users contact the help desk or security desk, if one exists. Detective capabilities trigger alerts, and outside entities, such as law enforcement, contact entities when evidence of a potential event are uncovered.

The early stages of an event are critical. When the moment comes, kicking off an investigation fluidly and without confusion is a must. Ignoring an alert or not following the correct process causes ineffectiveness. This is where the playbooks come in. No matter what type of event is taking place, a documented process should exist to conduct initial triage and any necessary escalation.

Triaging the event is important. Initial investigations focus on understanding if events are benign or part of a malicious campaign. Events of low consequence should be closed by the help or security desk without fanfare. Significant events are escalated for further analysis. Successful completion of these steps leads to successful responses.

Playbooks are most effective during the initial stages of event investigation, when impacts and escalation points are easily understood. The criteria used to spell out the impact must be present. The impact might include the following criteria to understand the impact level:

- Sensitivity of the assets involved in the event

- Impact to business operations and ability to recover

- Financial impact not related to downtime and lost productivity

The impact level derives from the considerations discussed here. If operations are impacted, the time required to restore them influences impact. Sensitive assets, such as customer data, intellectual property or confidential data, can be high-impact targets. Events causing legal fees and reputational damage are also examples of high-impact issues.

The overall severity of the event is based on how widespread the issue is. This is also specific to the event the playbook is addressing. For malware outbreaks, the size of the event might be based on number of machines affected. Some entities might measure number and types of machines affected. Compromised credentials would be looked at another way. For example, whether the credentials are privileged or not and how many credentials have been compromised should be considered. Table 7-4 shows an example of impacts resulting from a ransomware attack.

Table 7-4. *Data Impacts in This Example Are Measured on Three Levels*

Rating	Definition
High	Sensitive production data is impacted.
Medium	Production data in less sensitive environments is impacted.
Low	Data impacted is not sensitive.

Ransomware outbreaks are trouble when production environments are involved. Some data instances have longer restoration times and do not cause issues when data is inaccessible. Impact to sensitive data environments creates negative consequences almost immediately. Nonsensitive data locations are of lower impact to the entity, mainly owing to the time it takes the IT team to restore this data. The definitions are based on the risk tolerance of an organization. Entities with less risk tolerance might consider the unsuccessful targeting of end users with ransomware a low-impact event. Others barely consider it an event.

Once the impact is known, follow-up actions are required. The incident response plan dictates what to do next. High- and medium-impact events should be escalated to the incident response leader. The correct playbook should be utilized and the incident response plan followed. Low-impact incidents might be handled at the security or help desk level, with communication to the incident response leader required.

Summary

Identification is the first step in responding to events and incidents. Detective capabilities built within the entity provide the identification. End users detect suspicious activities and alert cybersecurity personnel, but technological capabilities provide much of the means used for identification. Entities of the smallest size often deal with large volumes of data, so much that it becomes necessary to automate to analyze data and correlate events. Mature security programs gather data from many sources, such as

- Applications and application servers

- Firewalls

- Intrusion detection and prevention systems

- Packet captures

- End point detection and response

- DNS security monitoring

- DLP solutions

- EDR solutions

- Infrastructure (operating systems and databases)

Data needs a place to go and a way for analysis to occur. Security events spawn many indicators. These indicators may make it obvious that an attack is occurring, and others may be only hinting at this. The increased use of SIEM solutions was designed to identify all the subtle hints of an attack and alert cybersecurity teams. These represent just some of the capabilities organizations need to implement to identify potential security incidents.

CHAPTER 8

Containment

Containment comes after identifying an event and concluding that action is required to limit its impact. Entities must understand the fundamentals of containment, the steps necessary to gather information on the event's characteristics, and how to identify the population of affected systems and users and quarantine those systems until the situation is resolved and business is back to normal. These actions are undertaken by internal resources or outside experts. A strategy built around objectives drives containment. The common approach is to identify the symptoms, quarantine the systems, and get back to business as soon as possible. Some approaches seek to confirm attribution to specific attack groups and monitor the attacker's movements. Another strategy is to quickly identify all affected systems and prepare each for eradication. There may be some cases in which following an attacker's movements is prudent, but for many organizations, the risk of observing and not acting is high.

Containment works best when the incident response team knows its actions and references playbooks and checklists for guidance. Establishing fundamental action plans using playbooks is important. At a minimum, playbooks for addressing malware, denial of service, lost assets, data theft and unauthorized use or misuse of assets are important. Teams must also manage executive expectations during this time. Focus is necessary to identify the indicators of events and catch all systems affected. It is reasonable to keep leadership updated on progress and next steps but not to speculate or attempt to draw conclusions without complete information.

Indicators of Compromise

Indicators of compromise are artifacts and evidence observed inside information systems confirming the existence of attacker actions. These indicators of compromise (IOCs) include virus signatures, changes to file systems and registries and outbound and inbound connections to and from known malicious URLs and domains, to name a few.

© Eric C. Thompson 2018

Threat intelligence documenting indicators from known threat groups adds context to investigations. When indicators point to potential threat actors as the source of an attack, the response team may be able to quickly ascertain the systems affected, by searching for the known indicators of that group.

Containment Fundamentals

Containment is about limiting the damage done by attackers. This is achieved by keeping the attacker away from key assets not yet compromised. Containing an event or incident requires identifying indicators of the attack and identifying them in other systems. Early in the process, initial indicators are the focus. Once a system is suspected of being compromised, it should be isolated. Some ways to do this include

- Unplugging the network cable

- Putting the machine in sleep mode (Powering it off causes volatile memory loss and the loss of forensic evidence.)

- Isolating the machine, so that it cannot receive data via changes to DNS and firewall rules

After the systems are isolated, images should be taken for use during the investigation. As those images are analyzed, identification and imaging of other affected systems are completed as well. As more and more systems are taken offline, productivity issues will ensue, and communication with the business is vital. Several open source and commercial solutions are available, such as Volatility, Rekal, and EnCase. File system and memory images are key here.

Once all identified systems are imaged, the response team correlates the data from each to further identify IOCs not yet investigated. The response team's goal is to identify as comprehensive a list of affected systems as possible. Attribution is not always necessary. In fact, for most entities, it is the last thing the response team should focus on. The focus should first be to contain the event and prepare for eradication.

Choosing a Containment Strategy

If incident response objectives are to identify, contain, and eradicate incidents as quickly as possible before any damage is done to sensitive data assets, what is the strategy for doing this? First, entities must assess the capabilities for containing events and incidents once they are identified. Small and medium-size organizations possess limited resources for responding properly to events, identifying indicators, uncovering them in information systems, and taking forensic images. These are specialized skills not often possessed internally. The strategy discussed in Chapter 5 engages outside entities to monitor detective capabilities such as data loss prevention, log correlation and security event management solutions. The strategy starts with identifying the event, working in concert with the third parties providing support to identify the IOCs and searching through the environment to locate other end points at which these indicators are present. The strategy then dictates eradicating the event and restoring systems, topics covered in Chapter 9.

The examples below outline specific types of containment but are not all-encompassing. Not every attack requires its own playbook, for example, attacks against a web application or server. The threat actor may exploit a vulnerability and gain access to the application or server. During the attack, the adversary may use rootkits, malware, and other tools to move laterally, elevate privileges, and maintain persistence. Playbooks may exist for the malware, rootkits, and unauthorized use of elevated privileges, but documentation about responding to web attacks or specific web vulnerabilities may not exist. A forensic investigation would lead to the web vulnerability as the source of the attack, with remediation occurring during the recovery phase.

Malware and Ransomware Outbreaks

Examples of containment activities specific to malware and ransomware outbreaks are highlighted in Figure 8-1.

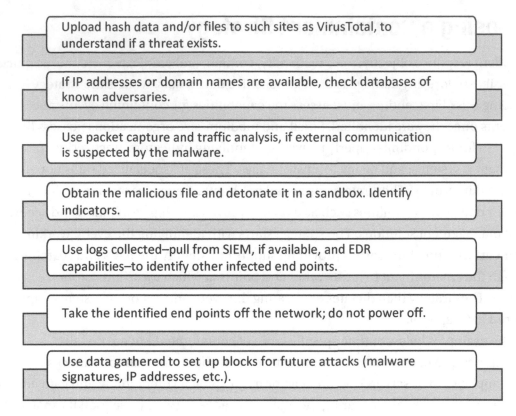

Upload hash data and/or files to such sites as VirusTotal, to understand if a threat exists.

If IP addresses or domain names are available, check databases of known adversaries.

Use packet capture and traffic analysis, if external communication is suspected by the malware.

Obtain the malicious file and detonate it in a sandbox. Identify indicators.

Use logs collected—pull from SIEM, if available, and EDR capabilities—to identify other infected end points.

Take the identified end points off the network; do not power off.

Use data gathered to set up blocks for future attacks (malware signatures, IP addresses, etc.).

Figure 8-1. *Typical steps taken to contain malware and ransomware outbreaks*

When notification of malware or ransomware is received, the incident response team must verify if a threat really exists. This could be a false positive, older malware not posing a threat to the entity, or malware from an active threat actor meant to be malicious. If the incident responders have the sample available, there are several ways to determine if a threat may exist. Databases such as VirusTotal allow users to upload attachments, hashes, and Universal Resource Locators (URLs) to get results based on others' experiences. Figures 8-2 through 8-7 display sample results of a file uploaded to VirusTotal for the Locky Ransomware strain. The images show the initial report on the file uploaded and an analysis of Locky behavior.

54 engines detected this file		
SHA-256	6bd1021e112a72e751f851da4c705100ebce5baf1d4d456ee64ab2edd768a54f	
File name	CAED44A5A63F09D1774E2D856BDFB81D.exe	
File size	617 KB	
Last analysis	2018-05-15 00:05:52 UTC	
Community score	-48	

54 / 66

Detection   Details   Relations   Behavior   Community ②

Ad-Aware	⚠ Trojan.Ransom.CerberKD.12369432	AegisLab	⚠ Ransom.Cerber.Smaly0!c
AhnLab-V3	⚠ Win-Trojan/Lukitus3.Exp	ALYac	⚠ Trojan.Ransom.LockyCrypt
Antiy-AVL	⚠ Trojan/Win32.TSGeneric	Arcabit	⚠ Trojan.Ransom.CerberKD.DBCBE18
Avira	⚠ TR/Crypt.ZPACK.tfrzh	AVware	⚠ Trojan.Win32.Generic!BT
Babable	⚠ Malware.HighConfidence	Baidu	⚠ Win32.Trojan.WisdomEyes.16070401....
BitDefender	⚠ Trojan.Ransom.CerberKD.12369432	Bkav	⚠ HW32.Packed.95D9
CAT-QuickHeal	⚠ Ransom.Exxroute.A4	ClamAV	⚠ Win.Trojan.Agent-6429700-0
Comodo	⚠ Backdoor.Win32.Tofsee.GN	CrowdStrike Falcon	⚠ malicious_confidence_100% (W)
Cyren	⚠ W32/Trojan.YFAB-9001	eGambit	⚠ Unsafe.AI_Score_65%
Emsisoft	⚠ Trojan.Ransom.CerberKD.12369432 (B)	Endgame	⚠ malicious (high confidence)
eScan	⚠ Trojan.Ransom.CerberKD.12369432	ESET-NOD32	⚠ Win32/Filecoder.Locky.L
F-Prot	⚠ W32/Ransom.FG.gen!Eldorado	F-Secure	⚠ Trojan.Ransom.CerberKD.12369432
Fortinet	⚠ W32/Injector.DRQA!tr	GData	⚠ Win32.Trojan.Kryptik.IS

Figure 8-2. *Image of initial results of Locky Ransomware analysis available at*
VirusTotal.com

Figure 8-2 shows the results of the Locky Ransomware analysis. These results, based on the last analysis of Locky on May 15, 2018, show that 54 of 66 virus engines detected this as malicious. The results for the first 26 engines are shown in Figure 8-2, and the remaining 44 are displayed in Figure 8-3.

Σ | Search or scan a URL, IP address, domain, or file hash

F-Prot	⚠ W32/Ransom.FG.gen!Eldorado	F-Secure	⚠ Trojan.Ransom.CerberKD.12369432
Fortinet	⚠ W32/Injector.DRQA!tr	GData	⚠ Win32.Trojan.Kryptik.IS
Ikarus	⚠ Trojan-Ransom.Locky	Jiangmin	⚠ Trojan.Refinka.it
K7AntiVirus	⚠ Trojan (0051918c1)	K7GW	⚠ Trojan (0051918c1)
Kaspersky	⚠ HEUR:Trojan.Win32.Generic	Malwarebytes	⚠ Ransom.Locky
MAX	⚠ malware (ai score=100)	McAfee	⚠ Ransomware-GFC!CAED44A5A63F
McAfee-GW-Edition	⚠ BehavesLike.Win32.Generic.jc	Microsoft	⚠ Ransom:Win32/Locky.A
NANO-Antivirus	⚠ Trojan.Win32.Cryptor.esqyfn	Palo Alto Networks	⚠ generic.ml
Panda	⚠ Trj/CI.A	Qihoo-360	⚠ HEUR/QVM19.1.CF9A.Malware.Gen
SentinelOne	⚠ static engine - malicious	Sophos AV	⚠ Mal/Elenoocka-E
Sophos ML	⚠ heuristic	Symantec	⚠ Ransom.Locky.B
Tencent	⚠ Win32.Trojan.Filecoder.Tcmf	TrendMicro	⚠ Ransom_CERBER.SMALY0
TrendMicro-HouseCall	⚠ Ransom_CERBER.SMALY0	VBA32	⚠ Trojan-Ransom.Cryptor
VIPRE	⚠ Trojan.Win32.Generic!BT	Webroot	⚠ W32.Trojan.Gen
Yandex	⚠ Trojan.Filecoder!I9Y7uOXgPVY	Zillya	⚠ Trojan.Cryptor.Win32.169
ZoneAlarm	⚠ HEUR:Trojan.Win32.Generic	Zoner	⚠ Trojan.Locky
Alibaba	✅ Clean	Avast	✅ Clean
Avast Mobile Security	✅ Clean	AVG	✅ Clean
CMC	✅ Clean	Kingsoft	✅ Clean
nProtect	✅ Clean	Rising	✅ Clean
SUPERAntiSpyware	✅ Clean	TheHacker	✅ Clean
TotalDefense	✅ Clean	ViRobot	✅ Clean
Cybereason	⊘ Unable to process file type	Symantec Mobile Insight	⊘ Unable to process file type
Trustlook	⊘ Unable to process file type		

Figure 8-3. *Results for the remaining 44 engines, from the VirusTotal analysis of Locky Ransomware*

Figures 8-4 to 8-7 show the results of the behavior analysis tab. Figure 8-4 displays network connections using HTTP, TCP, and UDP connections.

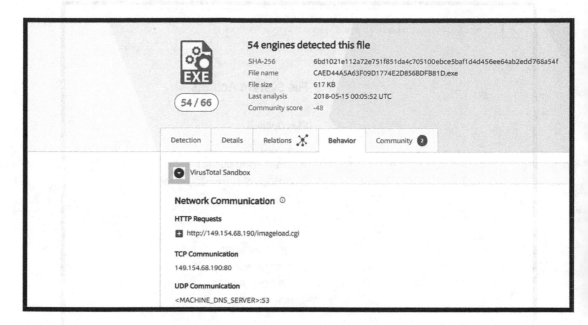

Figure 8-4. *Network communications identified by VirusTotal for the Locky Ransomware malware*

VirusTotal shows Locky connections to 149.154.68.190 using HTTP and 149.154.68.190:80 on TCP. The UDP connection attempts to connect to the DNS server on port 53.

Figure 8-5 displays the files opened and files read by Locky.

Figure 8-5.   *Files opened and read by Locky and identified by VirusTotal*

Locky opens several files, notably systems files. It also reads several systems files and several in the Python library. These are indicators the incident response team can use.

Figure 8-6 shows snippets of files written and files moved by Locky. Because the ransomware is Python-based, these files are all Python as well.

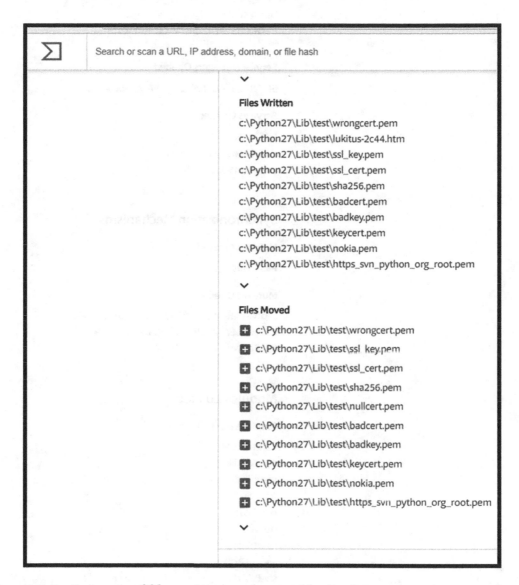

Figure 8-6. *Snippets of files written and moved by Locky*

Figure 8-7 shows the process and service actions executed by Locky and the modules loaded by the ransomware.

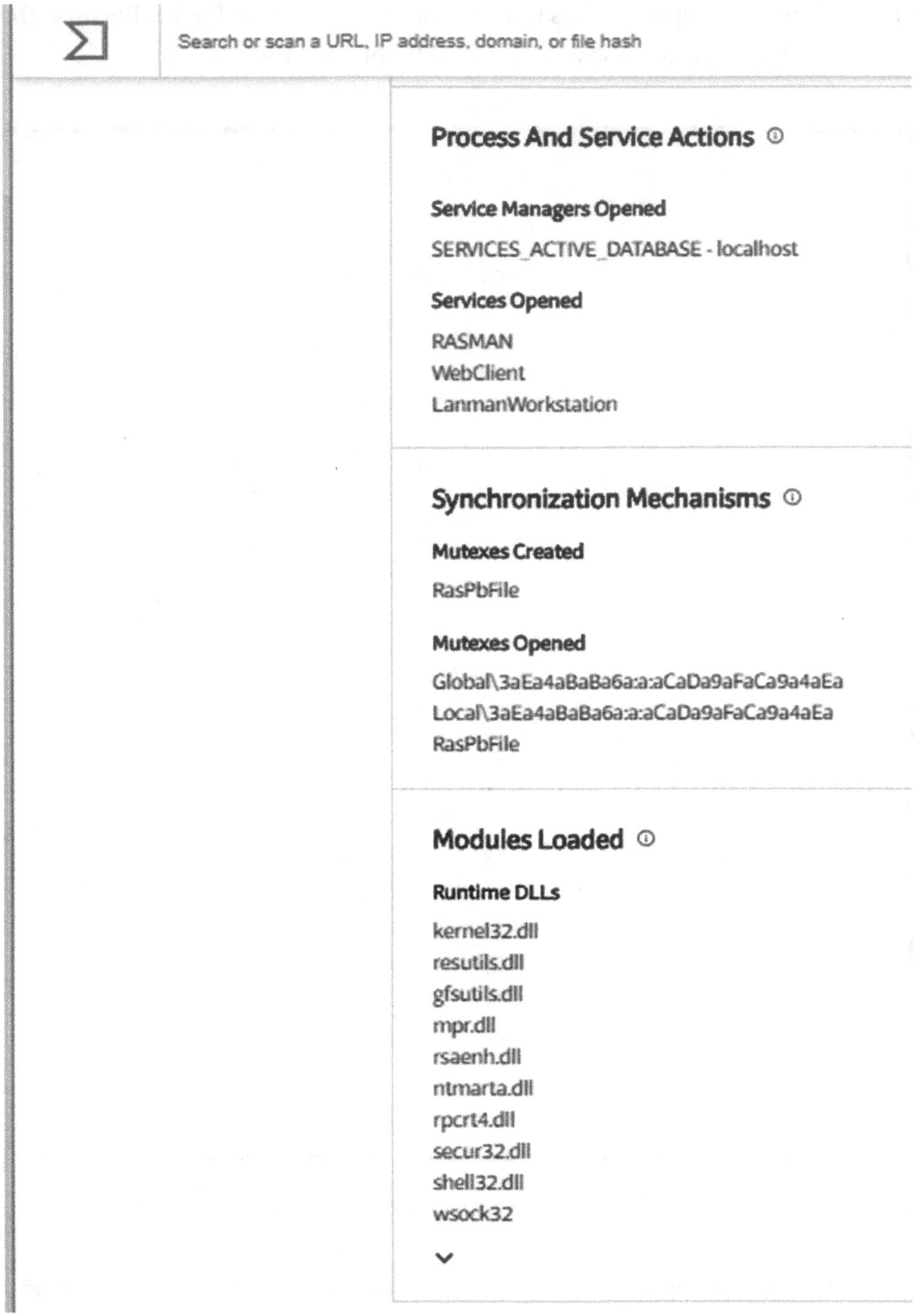

Σ   Search or scan a URL, IP address, domain, or file hash

Process And Service Actions ⓘ

Service Managers Opened

SERVICES_ACTIVE_DATABASE - localhost

Services Opened

RASMAN
WebClient
LanmanWorkstation

Synchronization Mechanisms ⓘ

Mutexes Created

RasPbFile

Mutexes Opened

Global\3aEa4aBaBa6a:a:aCaDa9aFaCa9a4aEa
Local\3aEa4aBaBa6a:a:aCaDa9aFaCa9a4aEa
RasPbFile

Modules Loaded ⓘ

Runtime DLLs

kernel32.dll
resutils.dll
gfsutils.dll
mpr.dll
rsaenh.dll
ntmarta.dll
rpcrt4.dll
secur32.dll
shell32.dll
wsock32

⌄

Figure 8-7. *The process and service actions of Locky and modules loaded, snippet only, for Locky*

Locky opened the SERVICES_ACTIVE_DATABASE - localhost service manager and the RASMAN, WebClient, and LanmanWorkstation services.

Caution   Attachments uploaded to VirusTotal for scanning are kept in the database. Be careful of what is uploaded, because the contents of the documents uploaded are publicly available.

Uploading the file or executable normally allows VirusTotal to provide associated domain names or IP addresses, if available. VirusTotal also lets you upload domain names and IP addresses for analysis. Learning the domain where the malware originated might lead to detecting command and control (C2) traffic, or, at least, equip the entity to block those domains and IPs from further communication inside the organization. Malware often communicates externally to C2 servers. These servers deliver instructions to the malware at specific intervals, based on call-backs to the C2 server. Detecting the history of calls to C2 sites by the malware is possible with packet capture software such as WireShark. WireShark is an open source tool with many features for capturing and analyzing traffic for investigative purposes. The key to detecting C2 communication is knowing what to look for, based on the initial analysis of the malware. In its article "Detecting and Analyzing Locky Ransomware," Digital Guardian displayed the malicious domain and IP used by the ransomware to download the malicious executable file 765f46vb.exe.[1] Once initiated, Locky connected to 177.185.194.115, `http://comprecaldas.com`. No matter the tool utilized, tying these indicators back to machines making connections helps the incident response team detect other infected machines on the network.

Entities with a sandbox environment can also detonate the malware and document its behaviors. Some well-crafted samples sense when a virtual environment is being used and will not execute, preventing incident response teams from learning the characteristics of the sample. If successful, dynamically analyzing the malware sample elicits real-time indicators of events when end points are affected, including

- Are files created and deleted?

- Are registry changes made?

- Does the malware attempt to connect outside the network?

---

[1] Patrick Upatham and Andy Passidomo, "Detecting and Analyzing Locky Ransomware with Digital Guardian (Screenshot Demo)," `https://digitalguardian.com/blog/detecting-and-analyzing-locky-ransomware-digital-guardian-screenshot-demo`, September 1, 2017.

Microsoft Sysinternals RegShot, ProcMon, and Process Monitor dynamically analyze malware behavior. Each is available as an open source solution, and all are common tools available to individuals requiring low-cost ways to conduct dynamic malware analysis. Table 8-1 outlines the purpose of each tool.

Table 8-1. *Four Tools Commonly Used to Conduct Dynamic Analysis of Malware*

Tool	Purpose
ProcMon	A.k.a. Process Monitor, this tool is available through Microsoft Sysinternals and monitors file system and service behavior, noting any changes made by the malware.
RegShot	In Windows environments, RegShot takes before and after snapshots of the registry. Once the malware is detonated in the sandbox, a second snapshot is taken.
Process Explorer	Another free Microsoft tool, Process Explorer displays services and the associated dynamic link libraries (DLLs) attached.

Detonating malware in a sandbox running ProcMon captures file system changes made by the malware and the starting and stopping of services. RegShot highlights changes made to registry settings by the malware, and Process Explorer shows services running, such as those captured by ProcMon. However, there is one exception, analysts can review the DLLs attached to those services. DLLs are libraries used to share code among applications and programs in Windows. Malware uses DLLs the same way, and threat hunters identify DLLs used by malware can search for DLLs attached to the processes run by malware as additional means for confirming that a machine or system is affected by the attack.

Figure 8-8 shows an image with the information Process Monitor provides. Analysts see the process name, process ID (PID), operation, path, result, and details.

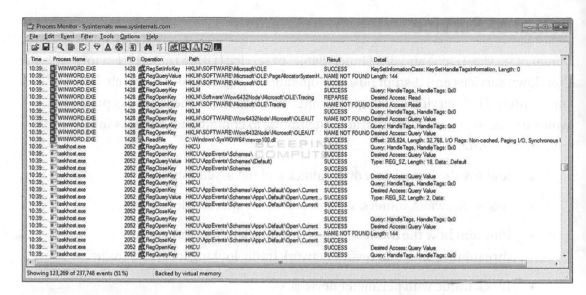

Figure 8-8. *Image displaying the screen contents when running Process Monitor. Executables initiated with Process Monitor live in a sandbox are beneficial to understanding what the executable does in the environment.*

If the malware is an executable, analysts observe the details for later use, searching for other instances of the malware in the environment. The processes in this example highlight numerous activities affecting the registry and one initiating a file read. The details lead analysts to further sources of investigation.

Commercial sandboxes are offered by several entities. Solutions often execute the malware in the sandbox and report the IOCs to the team. Teams do this manually or, when suspicious files traverse the network, they can be automatically detonated in the sandbox, with results sent to analysts.

Once the malware is examined and all indicators of compromise are documented, the incident response team can get down to finding all affected end points. If available, end point detection and response (EDR) SIEM and packet capture sources are used to inventory all affected devices.

Denial of Service

Denial of service (DoS) and distributed denial of service (DDoS) attacks aim to shut down services and disrupt business operations. The attacks target web-facing applications, DNS services, and egress points. Responding to these attacks properly avoids unnecessary availability issues. Attempting to contain these attacks involves the following important steps:

- Identify the logical flow of the attack and the assets targeted.

- Assess firewalls, routers, servers, and other affected device logs.

- Pinpoint how the traffic for the DDoS attack differs from non-threatening ones and review network traffic looking for DDoS traffic.

- Block traffic with perimeter devices.

- Block outbound traffic responding to the DDoS.

- Blackhole malicious IPs attributed to the attacker.

- Temporarily disable applications and services affected by the attack.

- Add servers and load balancers, as needed.

The response team can also contact the Internet service provider to confirm if it sees the attack. If so, it may aid in thwarting the adversary.

Lost Assets

Assets can be misplaced or stolen by end users and employees, and when these events occur, several questions must be answered. Assets in question here include laptops, tablets, mobile phones, desktops, printers, hard drives, and other types of removable or portable storage. Again, this list is not exhaustive, but focuses on common assets posing risks when not within the organization's grasp.

- If theft occurred, was a law enforcement report filed?

- What types of data were stored on the asset?

- What was the asset used for?

- Can the asset be tracked, wiped remotely, or can it call home?

These questions determine what risk exists due to the lost asset and the steps necessary to contain. If the asset was stolen, the matter should be reported to the police. More important is what data was stored on the asset. Concern arises when electronic protected health information (ePHI), personally identifiable information (PII), or confidential data the entity does not want made public were stored on the asset. If the asset was encrypted and powered down when possession was lost, the risks of data exposure are reasonably low. Some entities can track certain assets and/or wipe the contents remotely. These protections also reduce the risks of data exposure. If the company is uncertain whether sensitive data was stored on the asset, or if it was used in sensitive functions, monitoring the situation internally and externally is the extent of what the incident response team can do.

Data Theft

One of the worst situations an incident response team can find itself in is containing data theft. These events are newsworthy and require the team to catch up in a hurry. Indicators of data theft are obvious; others are subtler. Figure 8-9 highlights examples of each.

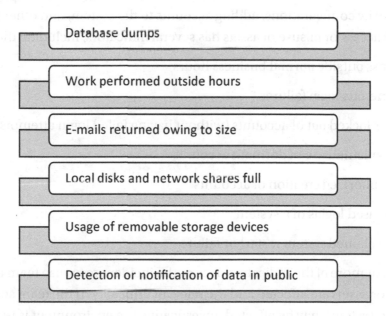

Figure 8-9. Sample indicators of data theft

The context of these warning signs is key to understanding the impact of the situation. Attacks on databases housing sensitive information, PII, ePHI, intellectual property, and trade secrets are serious. The same goes for alerts resulting from full disk space. If this situation occurs on infrastructure hosting sensitive data types, impact could be more significant. Further investigation is required because data can be moved from sensitive locations to less sensitive locations before exfiltration outside the entity boundaries.

User-based alerts, e-mails returned for size, working outside normal hours, and use of removable storage, which should be restricted to a select few, necessitate investigation of the user's access rights. Immediately understanding the class of assets at risk is important. Users with access to the data types previously mentioned pose the biggest threat to the entity.

Unauthorized Access and Misuse of Assets

End users can be tempted to do things that violate information security policies. This is done for personal reasons, wanting to use company assets for inappropriate means. Others do not appreciate the limits the information security teams place on them and desire ways to circumvent controls. Examples include misusing administrative privileges to change security configurations, adding accounts to the system, and other infractions. Unauthorized access or misuse of assets has several indicators, including the following:

- Access outside normal business hours

- Numerous login failures

- Users locked out of accounts (without having failed login attempts)

- Unexplained use of dormant accounts

- Unauthorized creation of accounts

- Increased logins of a system

- Unexplained system restart or failure

When one or more of the indicators occurs, the incident response team considers what systems or assets are affected and the relevant criticality. If the team suspects other end points and systems may be affected, investigating the environment is required. The team must know what servers, desktops, laptops, and mobile devices are affected. Are these directory accounts or accounts local to the device? These details address the impact of the scenario.

Retaining Forensic Investigators

Throughout the response, the team must gather digital evidence, to understand what happened. Some of this evidence is used to identify other compromised systems, and some is used to understand how the attack occurred. Images of systems in question are obtained by the incident response team. There are numerous commercial and open source tools to conduct these tasks, but, as discussed earlier in this chapter, the skills are not often found internally.

Retaining an incident response firm prior to an incident is ideal when you know the capabilities to respond do not exist on the team. These experts have experience containing incidents and collecting forensic evidence in response to cyberattacks. Depending on the agreement, the expected level of service might place the team on-site within 24 hours, or it could be that experts promise best efforts to place a team on-site as soon as possible. During large outbreaks, such as WannaCry, best efforts may mean days or weeks before response help arrives. Attention to these details is necessary, to make sure the required response times are built into the agreement.

Once a firm is engaged, on-site workshops and walkthroughs teach the entity's local IR team what to expect when calling the firm for assistance, expectations for deploying forensic tools in the environment, and opportunities for improvement that the forensic firm identified during these discussions. IR teams must be prepared to rapidly deploy forensic tools used by these firms and plan to gather the necessary approvals to do so.

Executive Expectations

One obstacle the incident response team will face during the containment phase results from executives and members of the business wanting rapid answers and conclusions. This is understandable. Business repercussions may be looming, and leaders want to get in front of any negative situations. The incident response team must stay focused on the task at hand, sharing relevant information when possible, updating leaders on the steps taken and planned, but resisting incomplete or speculative information just to appease the audience. Doing the latter can cause more harm later.

Summary

Containment requires an organization to collect indicators of compromise. Indicators are attributions and artifacts left behind during events. Threat actors have specific attributes, based on tools, techniques, and procedures used. Specific types of malware or ransomware make changes to systems the incident response team uses to search the remaining information systems and assets. When matches to the indicators hit, the incident response team can quarantine these systems, taking them offline for further analysis.

The process of gathering an initial set of indicators and searching for signs of each in the remaining systems are documented in playbooks used by the response team. Playbooks are specific to event types: malware/ransomware, denial of service, lost assets, data theft and unauthorized use or misuse of company assets. This is not a complete list, but very common scenarios seen by incident response teams.

During the containment phase, forensic evidence used to determine the root cause and how the event unfolded is also gathered. Images of the systems are captured for complete analysis of all system characteristics as part of containment.

During this time, incident response teams deal with contact from members of the business and company leadership seeking answers. This is to be expected. The organization could be impacted, depending on the severity of the events in question, and these groups have a need to know. The key is to give facts and not speculate. Speculation causes more harm than good.

CHAPTER 9

Eradication, Recovery, and Post-incident Review

Eradication is the process of removing all the remnants of a cyberattack. This commences once systems known to be compromised are available to be taken offline so that eradication can occur. Removing files and reversing registry and configuration changes malware and attackers made during the attack are addressed. Once all the affected machines are identified and isolated and forensic backups are completed, the company can address weaknesses exploited by the attackers. These vulnerabilities are patched, and insecure configurations repaired. In some cases, reimaging machines is the best course of action to ensure that the presence of the attack is removed. This is often true when rootkits are involved. Once completed, systems can be brought back online. As systems are restored the environment is monitored for indicators of the attack reemerging. If indicators resurface, incident responders go back to the drawing board and use playbooks to address containment through recovery again. The final phase is to conduct the post-incident review for lessons learned. These meetings are necessary to discuss what went well during the response to ensure that good behavior continues and that improvements needed secure the effective operation of the program.

Removing the Attacker's Artifacts

Once systems are taken offline, incident responders and members of the information technology team focus on eradicating the remnants of the attack and bringing those systems back online. Figure 9-1 displays the types of attacks discussed and responded to through various playbooks and steps taken to eradicate the affects.

117

E. C. Thompson, *Cybersecurity Incident Response*, https://doi.org/10.1007/978-1-4842-3870-7_9

Malware and Ransomware

- Delete files (created, modified, and hidden).
- Remove file changes.
- Reverse registry changes.

Denial of Service

- Update rule sets in firewalls and intrusion prevention systems.
- Implement new technology, if necessary, to prevent future attacks of the same pattern.

Rootkits

- Locate original image of machine.
- Reimage machine and build the OS from scratch.

Figure 9-1. *Examples of eradication techniques used for various types of attacks against the entity*

One other item to consider is changing the name of the system, IP addresses, and domain name system (DNS).[1] These actions are taken if a concern over copycat attacks exists. This decision makes sense when the benefits of making the change outweigh the risks of changing systems in production.

Malware Artifacts

Formerly, some antivirus solutions removed files and fixed changes made to operating systems by malicious software. This was common when signature-based detection was the norm. While those days are not completely over, at present, malware used by attackers is known to be signatureless and able to avoid detection. This makes removing malware artifacts tougher because identifying the changes made by malicious software takes time and attention to detail. If the malware strain has a history of use, IOCs and other intelligence direct eradication activities to specific folders and system changes.

---

[1]Ed Skoudis and John Strand, *Incident Handling Step-by-Step and Computer Crime Investigation* (SANS, 2018).

Entities that know the services normally running on systems, with standard images and documented traffic patterns, find this step easier than entities without this information.

In February 2018, Bitdefender ranked the top-ten malware threats of 2017.[2] One interesting item on the list is the fourth most common threat, the Downadup worm, also known as W32.Downadup and Conficker. It is an old strain, first detected in 2008, but unpatched systems are still vulnerable to it. In its article on how to eradicate this adversarial worm, Symantec[3] states that it is one of the most sophisticated pieces of software, but one that has not changed much during its life. Like most malicious code, Conficker uses services present in the environment, specifically, Microsoft Windows Server Service RPC Handling Remote Code Execution Vulnerability. The article walks readers through the process of containing the outbreak, by identifying the indicators and searching through the network, as discussed in Chapter 8. In this case, the incident response team used Symantec's end point product to remove Downadup, by executing the following:

- Taking the machine offline by removing the network cable

- Booting the machine in safe mode

- Using the Downadup removal tool

- Rebooting the machine and confirming that the infection is gone

---

Note   This example uses Symantec's end point or the Downadup Removal Tool to eradicate the infection. Depending on the environment and capabilities, incident response teams go through similar processes to eradicate malware from end points. These processes differ, based on the many user solutions in the marketplace.

Once it has been confirmed that the malware is no longer present, the information security team monitors the end points affected, and the rest of the environment, for indications the malware persists.

---

[2]Bogdan Botezatu, "Bitdefender Ranks The Top 10 Malware Threats of 2017," Bitdefender, `https://businessinsights.bitdefender.com/bitdefender-ranks-the-top-10-malware-threats-of-2017`, February 12, 2018.

[3]Symantec, "Killing Conficker: How to Eradicate W32.Downadup for Good," `www.symantec.com/connect/articles/killing-conficker-how-eradicate-w32downadup-good`, January 31, 2014.

Rootkits

Attackers use rootkits to create back doors, a method to continually return and carry out malicious objectives. Attackers install rootkits by making changes to the file system, enabling persistence. Because such activity is privileged, attackers make sure evidence of the rootkit's existence is hidden, making rootkits a high-impact situation. In its article on rootkit threats and defending against them, eSecurity Planet[4] discussed the five types of rootkits listed in Figure 9-2.

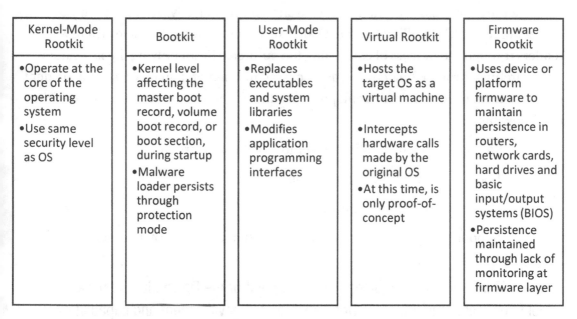

Kernel-Mode Rootkit	Bootkit	User-Mode Rootkit	Virtual Rootkit	Firmware Rootkit
•Operate at the core of the operating system •Use same security level as OS	•Kernel level affecting the master boot record, volume boot record, or boot section, during startup •Malware loader persists through protection mode	•Replaces executables and system libraries •Modifies application programming interfaces	•Hosts the target OS as a virtual machine •Intercepts hardware calls made by the original OS •At this time, is only proof-of-concept	•Uses device or platform firmware to maintain persistence in routers, network cards, hard drives and basic input/output systems (BIOS) •Persistence maintained through lack of monitoring at firmware layer

Figure 9-2. *Five common types of rootkits and associated behavior. Rootkits are often difficult to find, because they tend to blend in with services already running on the target system.*

Rootkits such as the preceding types are often hard to identify and, therefore, hard to remove, because each is designed to blend in with services already running on the system. Examples of rootkits in each of these categories include

- *Kernel-mode rootkit*: FU, Knark, Adore, Rkit, and Da IOS

- *Bootkits*: Olmasco, Rovnix, and Stoned Bootkit

---

[4]Fred Donovan, "Top 5 Rootkit Threats and How to Root Them Out," eSecurity Planet, www.esecurityplanet.com/network-security/top-5-rootkit-threats-and-how-to-root-them-out.html, November 9, 2016.

- *User-mode rootkit*: Vanquish, Aphex, and Hacker Defender
- *Firmware rootkit*: Cloaker and VGA rootkit

Often, when evidence exists confirming the use of rootkits by attackers, the best method for removing the rootkit and eliminating persistent access is restoring the system to its original state.

Vulnerability Scanning

Once all systems affected by the attack are remediated, the incident response team should scan the environment, confirming that the vulnerabilities mitigated are no longer present. Scanning the affected environment and documenting the results are necessary steps to show that no unmitigated vulnerabilities have been left behind.

Patching Vulnerabilities

During eradiation, emergency change requests should be processed and approved, so that patches and configuration changes are applied. These items should be documented in a change request and approved. The team must also retain copies of this documentation in the incident response report.

Restoring Systems via Backups

When restoration is the only answer to eradication, the incident response team often must work with the infrastructure team, to facilitate this process, once images of affected systems are captured. This removes anything left behind by the attackers.[5]

Post-incident Review

One of the most important and often forgotten elements of the incident response program and execution of the incident response plan is conducting lessons learned. Any time the plan is initiated, whether for a full-fledged incident, or investigating and

---

[5]Skoudis and Strand, *Incident Handling Step-by-Step and Computer Crime Investigation.*

triaging events, the opportunity to discuss the events as a team is an opportunity to learn about and improve responses. Upon reflection, it is inevitable that some elements of the response are identified as requiring changes. These can include

- Actions taken that are not documented in the incident response plan or requisite playbooks

- Actions team members forgot to perform

- Actions not documented that the team identified during execution

The goal at the end of the session is to document what went well and what opportunities for improvement exist. This is also a good time for the team to review preliminary drafts of the incident response report and provide input. The incident response leader must document the order of events and outcomes into an executive-level report for management review. This review of the incident and lessons learned is necessary for management to understand the incident response program's effectiveness and the necessary changes. This is done through the language in the report and tracking metrics such as

- Time to detect

- Time to respond

- Time to contain

- Time to eradicate

- Reoccurrence

Other examples exist. The main idea is that management and the incident response team must choose metrics that measure the behaviors and outcomes the company desires. The time-based measurements noted here are relevant to an entity desiring rapid response, containment, and eradication of incidents. Entities focused on identifying and prosecuting bad actors will choose different metrics, directed at those outcomes.

Summary

Eradication is the process of removing malicious artifacts from the environment. It also includes mitigating vulnerabilities exploited and other weaknesses, such as those exploited by the adversary. Recovery processes place systems back into production, in a stronger state, it is hoped. Updates to network hardware, additional patches, and configuration changes designed to strengthen the systems from future attacks are key. Finally, ensuring that the team sits down and goes over the event is important. This action is often missed. Entities do not find the time to go over the incident response process and document what was effective and what needs improvement. Common examples include updating the incident response plan or playbooks, to add or modify steps, and discussing behaviors and actions of the team, to reinforce expectations. The goal at the end of the eradication phase is documenting the incident and events in an executive report outlining actions taken, outcomes, and lessons learned, with metrics tracking activities directed at desired outcomes. Ultimately, management, or the body representing management as it relates to cybersecurity, must review the documentation and authorize necessary changes.

CHAPTER 10

Continuous Monitoring of Incident Response Program

An important characteristic of program maturity is continuous monitoring by management. This means leaders of the program establish performance indicators, aligned with management's expectations, and these indicators are reviewed regularly. In the Program Review for Information Security Assurance (PRISMA), these actions are captured in the measured and managed categories. Metrics are developed, and management reviews performance of the program, to confirm that it meets the organization's needs. The National Institute for Standards and Technology (NIST) special publication (SP) 800-137[1] was created to outline how federal agencies should develop continuous monitoring. These guidelines are useful for developing continuous monitoring inside any organization, and it is especially important for monitoring the performance of the incident response program. The key pieces of continuous monitoring include

- Defining a continuous monitoring strategy
- Establishing a continuous monitoring program
- Implementing the program
- Analyzing and reporting findings
- Responding to findings
- Reviewing and updating the strategy and program

---

[1]Kelley Dempsey et al., "Information Security Continuous Monitoring (ISCM) for Federal Information Systems and Organizations," NIST SP 800-137, September 2011.

So even here, where a process is established to continually monitor the security program and, more specifically, the incident response program, a step exists to review and update the program responsible for the review and update to key processes. This pushes the program toward a data-driven model. Evaluating performance against established benchmarks, adjusting where necessary, and monitoring progress period by period are keys to effectiveness.

In this scenario, in which the NIST Cybersecurity Framework was adopted as the foundation of the cybersecurity program, continuous monitoring focuses on the Detect, Respond, and Recover Functions.

To understand how to apply NIST (SP) 800-137, this chapter steps through the fundamental concepts and processes of continuous monitoring. Then these concepts are applied to the cybersecurity environment discussed in Chapters 2 and 3.

Components of Continuous Monitoring

All NIST publications, and (SP) 800-137 is no different, are ideal for laying the groundwork for effective development of processes and procedures. The need to monitor the incident response program is so important that beginning with an established foundation is necessary.

- Define a monitoring strategy.

- Establish the monitoring program.

- Implement the monitoring program.

- Analyze and report findings.

- Review findings.

- Review and update the continuous monitoring strategy.

NIST (SP) 800-137 aligns with the risk management program guidelines published in (SP) 800-37. The assumption is that a risk analysis and assessment were conducted, and the entity identified security measures to reduce risks to an acceptable level and is monitoring the operation of the security measures. This is the last step constituting risk management. Cyber risk managers select controls based on expected gains in risk reduction due to effective operation of security measures. The only way to know if these security measures are operating as expected is monitoring the control processes through various means discussed in this chapter. Detection, response, and recovery risks may be present, and controls are selected within these functions to reduce these risks. Examples of these include failure to detect malicious activity on end points, incident response plans not reviewed in a timely manner, and undocumented recovery processes, all of which can allow threat actors to successfully compromise the confidentiality, integrity, and availability of digital assets. When controls are put in place to address these issues, confirming that the controls are operating is necessary.

The Organizational Tiers

Special publication 800-137 divides entities into three tiers, as shown in Figure 10-1.

Figure 10-1. *Key audiences identified in NIST (SP) 800-137*

The members of these three focus areas view the data collected during continuous monitoring differently.

Tier 1—The Organization

Governance lives at the Organization tier. Policy- and strategy-related identification, mitigation, and monitoring of risks belong in Tier 1 and are communicated to Tiers 2 and 3. The metrics delivered to members of this tier are used to make decisions supporting risk management and governance of the entity.[2]

---

[2]Dempsey et al., pg. 8.

Tier 2—Mission and Business Critical

Members of management responsible for key business processes are accountable for mitigating risks affecting those processes.

Tier 3—Information System

This layer focuses on the information security controls implemented to reduce risks to the systems for which the entity depends. Special publication 800-137 specifically states the requirements at this tier to be security controls that are

- Implemented correctly

- Operate effectively

- Produce the desired outcome

NIST highlights security alerts, incidents occurred, and threat activity as metrics collected by Tier 3.

How Continuous Monitoring Works

The purpose of continuous monitoring is to guide the entity to make decisions based on risk.[3] For incident response, the goal is risk-based decision making based on the risks of not detecting events and insufficient responses to events. That means entities must test cybersecurity controls, understand the effectiveness of the controls and report on the effectiveness of the controls. This process works via the components identified previously that make up continuous response.

The Continuous Monitoring Strategy

Developing a continuous monitoring strategy is about nothing more than identifying the necessary data, frequency, and reporting methods for leaders at each tier, so that they can make decisions. Each tier may collect similar data and similar frequencies but it may also need additional information based on the requirements of the tier.

---

[3]Dempsey et al., pg. 16.

Tier 1 and Tier 2

The first two tiers, Organization and Mission and Business Critical, work closely together when defining the strategy. The leader in charge of making risk-based decisions at the organizational tier can be the same person who leads the governing body as it relates to information security. Organizations also develop information security steering committees to oversee the information security program. Here, the risk tolerance or acceptable risk levels are identified, policies are adopted and risk mitigation strategy is designed. The Mission and Business Critical tier often develops the procedures and processes meant to carry out the risk mitigation strategy, while collecting and reporting metrics based on the objectives outlined at the Organization tier. To facilitate the collection of data necessary to carry out the continuous monitoring strategy, key documentation is created at these two layers. Figure 10-2 shows the policy and procedural elements necessary to carry out the continuous monitoring strategy.

Key Policy and Procedure Elements

- Key Metrics
- Assessment of control effectiveness
- Status monitoring
- Reporting
- Assessing risk
- Configuration Management
- Frequency
- Sample Size and Population Requirement

Figure 10-2. *Policy and procedural elements necessary to implement the continuous monitoring strategy*

Tier 3

Here, at the system level, the security controls in place operate at all three levels. The data collected and used by the system is derived from system controls identified and placed into operation at Tiers 1 and 2. The Information System level implements the process and written procedures to meet the strategic objectives defined. These control processes, like all the other control process at each tier, are assessed for effectiveness, according to the risk management needs of the organization.

Incorporating Continuous Monitoring into the NIST CSF Environment

The guidelines outlined by NIST are valuable for entities wanting to monitor the environment and confirm that risk management objectives are being met. How does this look in the actual environment? Using the NIST CSF guidelines, monitoring for the purposes of incident response focuses on risks related to detecting, responding to, and recovering from incidents.

What Are the Incident Response Risks?

Chapter 6 discussed the role of preplanning in the incident response program. Plan development and response requires preplanning, focusing on risks to assets the entity deems important. One way to plan for an event is to analyze the risks to assets, which provide clues as to how an event may unfold in the environment.

Vulnerabilities in the Environment

What weaknesses does the entity have related to incident response? Table 10-1 lists several examples.

Table 10-1. *Identified Vulnerabilities Related to the Incident Response Program*

Immature end point detection capabilities
No packet capture solutions in place
No monitoring of egress points (places where data leaves the entity to outside locations)
Limited collection of logs and no central location for storage
Incident response plan not updated in a timely manner
Incident response team lacks business and executive representation

Risk statements for these vulnerabilities are documented in a risk register and should be measured based on severity. Most common is high, medium, or low severity ratings assigned to risks. Figure 10-3 lists risks statements, based on the vulnerabilities identified in Table 10-1.

Attacks by nation-states go undetected because end point detection capabilities do not exist.

Incident response teams cannot confirm attacks by nation-states, malicious outsiders, or malicious insiders because network traffic analysis cannot be performed.

Security operations personnel fail to detect data transmissions via egress points because egress points are not monitored.

Attacks by malicious outsiders cannot be investigated in a timely manner because logs are not collected and stored in a central repository.

Attacks by malicious insiders and outsiders have greater impact because the incident response plan is not updated in a timely manner.

Attacks by malicious insiders and outsiders have greater impact because senior management is not represented in the incident response process.

Figure 10-3. *Identified risks affecting desired outcomes of the incident response program*

Assigning Security Controls to Reduce the Risks

Once risks are identified, the next step is to assign security controls meant to reduce risks to an acceptable level. In this case, this means decreasing the risks of undesirable incident response outcomes. For entities, this means risks no greater than low, while other entities may accept moderate risks. Figure 10-4 shows control statements written to reduce risks to the incident response program.

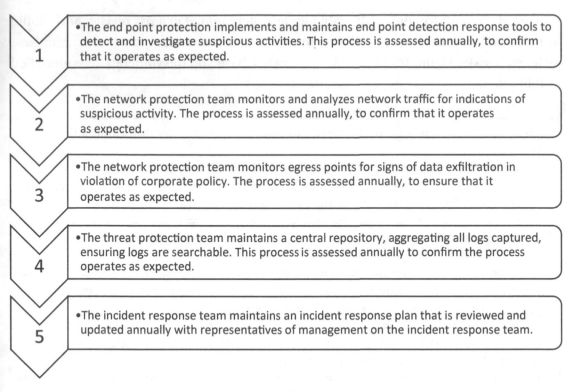

Figure 10-4. *Control statements written to reduce risks to the incident response program*

Defining the Monitoring Strategy

Developing a monitoring strategy for the incident response program focuses on assessing and measuring the controls assigned to reduce the detection, response, and recovery risks. Tier 1 (Organization) and Tier 2 (Mission and Business Critical) decide on many key components for monitoring these controls. Figure 10-5 shows these key decisions. This input allows the members at Tiers 1 and 2 to make decisions about the incident response controls and adjust, where necessary.

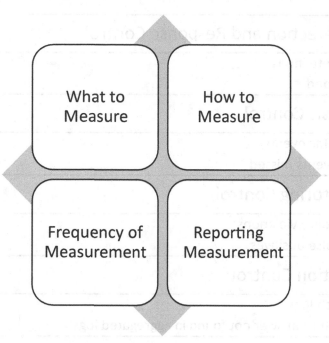

Figure 10-5. *Key decisions of the incident response program monitoring strategy*

Establishing and Implementing the Program

This phase requires the entity to assign individual responsibilities for each of the key strategic areas identified in Figure 10-3. The Organization tier establishes metrics with input from the other two tiers. Individual responsibility is assigned for assessment and reporting at the expected frequency.

Analyzing Data and Reporting Findings

Entities analyze and report assessment and monitoring results. These results let the Organization tier understand if the risks to the incident response program are managed properly. Figure 10-6 shows sample metrics and analysis for the incident response program controls.

> **End Point Detection and Response Control**
>
> • Number of detections
> • Time to respond

> **Traffic Analysis Control**
>
> • Malicious traffic events
> • Number of events missed

> **Egress Monitoring Control**
>
> • Number of policy violations
> • Number of false positives

> **Log Aggregation Control**
>
> • Time to search logs
> • Number of times answer not found in aggregated logs

> **Incident Response Plan Control**
>
> • How often is the plan updated?
> • How many updates are made?

Figure 10-6. *Examples of metrics analyzed by the Organization, Mission and Business Critical, and Information System tiers*

Responding to Findings

Security-related information collected during monitoring must be responded to. If the time to respond to end point protection events is not satisfactory, the entity adjusts the control process. Perhaps the control needs to be executed by other teams or individuals, or the process should be outsourced. It could be that the capability implemented needs adjustments, to operate effectively. The organization executes this process for each incident response control process.

Reviewing and Updating the Monitoring Program

Reviewing the monitoring program involves taking stock of the metrics gathered and understanding what the metrics mean to the incident response program.

- Are the right metrics assessed?

- Is the frequency sufficient?

- Is the right information reported?

Where the answers to these questions are no, adjustments are made to the program.

Summary

The incident response program requires effective monitoring to ensure that the program meets the needs of the entity and continues to improve. Entities must identify risks associated with failures of the incident response program, to achieve desired outcomes. These outcomes normally are quick and efficient identification of undesirable events, containing these, eradicating them, and recovering when malicious behavior occurs. Risks of undesirable outcomes are reduced by using security controls and processes. These controls are monitored, based on identified metrics and are assessed at specific intervals. Organization, Business and Mission Critical, and Information System tier leaders assess these controls and report findings at each level. Analysis leads to adjusting the program, as necessary, if performance does not meet the entity's requirements. This continuous cycle of assessment, reporting, analysis and adjustment allows the incident response program to grow and operate effectively.

CHAPTER 11

Incident Response Story

Following is an incident response story. The principals are an initial response team (IRT); a supplemental initial response team (SIRT), which the Chief Information Security Officer (CISO) and Vice President (VP) of Infrastructure join when events are escalated; the IT and extended initial response team (EIRT), in addition to the CIO and General Counsel; and, finally, an Executive Team that becomes involved once it has been determined that an incident has occurred and business impacts are probable. The team, once alerted to the initial incident, is expected to follow the plan, execute specific playbooks, and communicate internally.

Background

A manufacturing company, American Widget, has several lines of business. The primary line, for which it is best known, is manufacturing high-end widgets. These widgets enjoy a reputation for high quality and cater to a small market, owing to their high price and specific use cases. The typical customer is a high-net-worth individual, with somewhere near $100 million in assets and sufficient cash flow to maintain the widget. Many widget customers are celebrities, including movie stars, rock stars, well-known businesspeople and a few politicians.

Although it has several units, the firm consists of two business units that generate revenue: Sales and Preferred Finances. Sales earns revenue through initial sales or trade-in upgrades to newer widgets. There is also a significant amount of service and maintenance required annually for each widget, and customers buy annual service packages to maintain these. Preferred Finances supports the rest of the business. Figure 11-1 shows the key players at American Widget that have a role in the incident response program, depending on the issues at stake. Each unit is led by a vice president and supported by several junior vice presidents, managers and team leaders. American Widget employs nearly 300 individuals. The company has two locations in the United

States, the headquarters and a distribution and delivery center. Manufacturing is in Mexico and the Philippines.

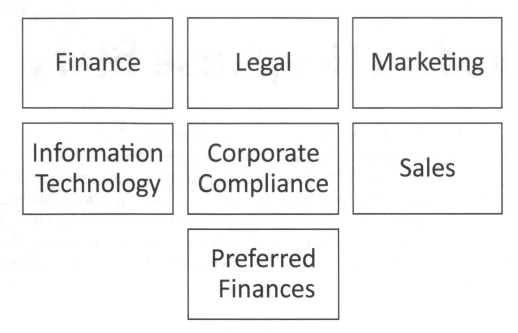

Figure 11-1. *The key business units involved in American Widget's incident response program*

Initial Response

The IRT is composed of six individuals, as outlined in Figure 11-2. This team is led by an Information Security Manager responsible for investigating events escalated by one of the security analysts.

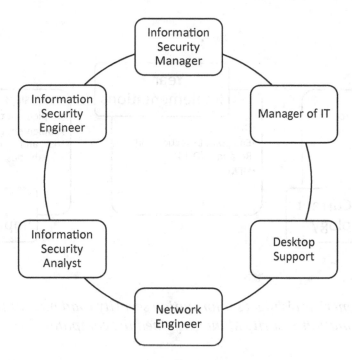

Figure 11-2. *Members of the initial response team*

The Manager of Information Security has a strong technical background. He began his career working as an entry-level network analyst and quickly fell in love with information security. He spent time as a security engineer, managing firewalls and then worked at a company managing security services for several entities. There, he implemented and managed data loss protection (DLP), firewalls, end point protection suites, and vulnerability management solutions. The CISO also has a strong technical background. Prior to assuming this role, she spent most of her career in security operations and network operations centers, monitoring the health of network equipment and conducting traffic analysis. Then she moved into security operations, focusing on helping organizations to capture log data and aggregate it in a central repository for correlation and analysis. She and the Information Security Manager were brought in to American Widget to close the large security gaps existing at the time. Only two years ago, American Widget did not have effective basic security technology. Firewall rules were stale, end point protection lacked the newest capabilities, and the ability to detect and respond to threats was nonexistent. Figure 11-3 outlines several of the more important implementations in the security road map.

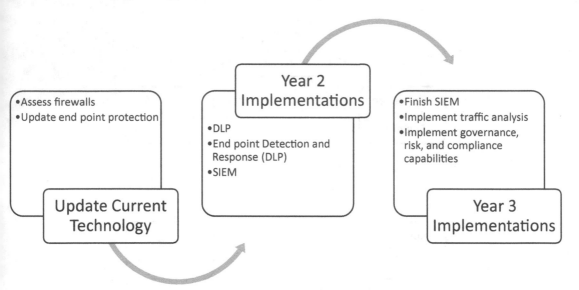

Figure 11-3. *American Widget's information security road map at the time the CISO and Information Security Manager joined the company*

Now, in year three, security incident and event management (SIEM) has been implemented and tools to capture and analyze traffic are now working. The CISO now plans to focus on hiring a new team member to focus on governance, risk and compliance. She feels this will round out the team and bring balance to the group. The Information Security Manager does not agree; he is more concerned with bringing in another engineer or technical analyst. He has visions of developing a team capable of threat hunting and conducting forensic examinations, reverse engineering malware, etc. The CISO is sticking to her guns. Policies are outdated, and American Widget is responsible for several areas of compliance, including PCI, and because of the lending it provides to most customers, several regulations apply to these services. Both the CISO and the Information Security Manager are not interested in this aspect of information security, and the only documentation completed during the past three years relate to procedures for operating the technology tools implemented and a one-page diagram of the incident response team.

The Nightmare Begins

This event began subtly. E-mails suggesting performance issues not seemingly related to one another were sent to the help desk. These events were not correlated, and details of each event were not shared with entire teams or across teams. It was not until much later in the event time line that the significant relationship of these events was known.

Blue Screen of Death

When the Information Security Manager sat down at his desk on a Wednesday morning, his inbox contained several messages he was copied on between a member of the Preferred Finance team and the Information Security Analyst. Apparently, the Preferred Finance Manager's computer kept getting a blue screen and crashing when he tried to open an e-mail from a key customer. The Information Security Manager did not understand why this was a security issue—desktop support owned these types of service issues. The Information Security Analyst informed the manager of the desktop group of the situation, guessing that there was a glitch in the hard drive. The Information Security Manager picked up the phone and called the Security Analyst. Despite his feeling that the issue fell under the purview of desktop support and not security, he decided it might be worth investigating.

"Good morning," the Security Analyst said, answering the call.

"Hey, this attachment crashing the computer, can you check it out and see if there is anything peculiar about it?"

"Don' you think it's just a flaky hard drive?" the analyst suggested.

"If it was the hard drive, the machine would not boot back up after it crashed. It is probably a desktop issue, but I would like you to take a look."

With that, the Information Security Manager hung up the phone.

A Locked Database

Not more than a minute later, a call came in from one of the VPs of Manufacturing. He informed the Information Security Manager that the database containing all the plans and images used to manufacture widgets was locked. The VP said one of his managers received an e-mail with a link to win a free vacation and clicked on it. The manager was redirected to a web site that displayed a 404 error indicating the destination was unreachable. Then, an e-mail was sent to the manager, stating that a specific database was encrypted, and American Widget must pay $1 million to get its data back. The Manager of Information Security told the VP he would call someone from the Infrastructure team and see if database restoration was possible with the latest backup.

The Manager of Information Security walked over to his counterpart in Infrastructure to discuss the locked database. He waited patiently at the Infrastructure manager's desk, listening to her talk to a sales manager about his laptop not working properly. She was obviously struggling to get this sales manager to let her transfer him to a desktop technician to work on the problem. When she hung up the phone, the Manager of Information Security gave her a minute to catch her breath. He felt it was important to play it cool, so when he gave her the news about the encrypted database and ransomware demand, he made sure to hide the panic he was feeling. While explaining the situation to the Infrastructure manager, the Information Security Manager emphasized the importance of quickly restoring the data. The last thing he needed to deal with was word that the plans used to manufacture American Widget's products were inaccessible, owing to a ransomware attack.

On his way back to his office, the Information Security Manager stopped by the Security Analyst's desk. He was concerned about the manufacturing database, so he asked her to work with the Infrastructure team and monitor the database restoration.

All Is Quiet

Within two days, the Infrastructure team restored the database, and manufacturing operations continued as planned. The Information Security Manager was relieved, thinking he had just dodged a bullet, but was proud of the company's response to the issue. Putting the Security Analyst on the job, had confirmed several facts during her research.

- The link came from an organization known to conduct ransomware attacks.

- This attack was different, because its source normally went after financial systems and focused on the financial industry.

Gathering these facts, the Information Security Manager decided to put together the time line of what occurred, so that he could show it to his boss. He developed the following slides to illustrate the attack. He broke it into the three phases, documented in Figure 11-4.

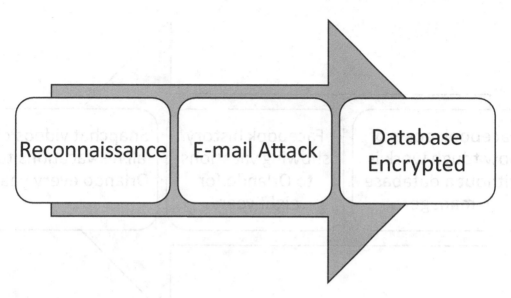

Figure 11-4. *The phases of the ransomware attack, as understood by the Information Security Manager*

Three weeks after the incident, the Information Security Manager sat down with the CISO to brief her on the incident regarding the manufacturing database. First, he took her through the reconnaissance phase and how he suspected the Manufacturing Manager was targeted and fell victim to the phishing e-mail. Figure 11-5 highlights the sequence of events used to social engineer the Manufacturing Manager and craft a targeted e-mail successfully designed to gain a foothold in the network.

Figure 11-5. *The sequence of social media sites attackers used to conduct reconnaissance on the Manufacturing Manager*

A cursory look at his profiles was all the attackers needed to learn that the Manufacturing Manager oversaw the widget design and build teams. Because they were Facebook friends, the Information Security Manager explained that he could view everything the Manufacturing Manager posted. The travel-related e-mail was not much harder to trace to the Manufacturing Manager either, as seen in Figure 11-6.

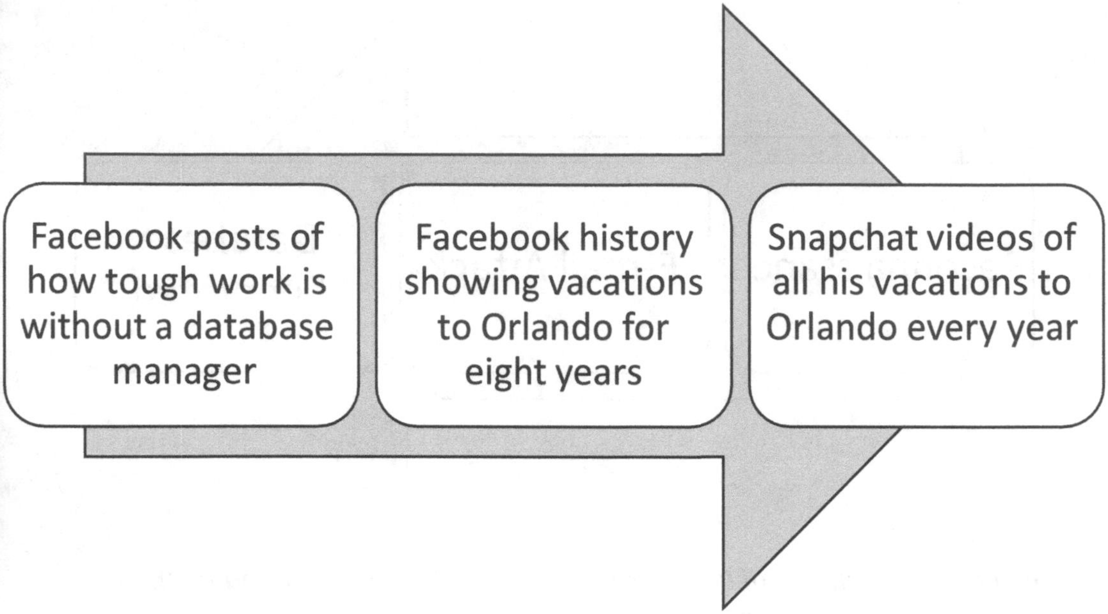

Figure 11-6. *Evidence found by the Information Security Manager during his review of social media posts*

The Information Security Manager explained to the CISO that the e-mail for a free vacation was the perfect ruse. Luckily, the backups were not corrupted, because they are kept offsite, and the database was restored without issue.

"Could you imagine if we did not have backups and lost all those manufacturing plans," the Information Security Manager said, feigning a shudder.

"It would not have caused a crisis," the CISO responded. "We file those plans with regulators for inspection purposes. We could have gotten the images back through e-mail archives, if all else failed."

The Information Security Officer left the meeting feeling less than spectacular. How could he not have known that?

The First Angry Call

Several months later, Client Services received an angry phone call from a well-known Hollywood director. She was livid.

"I just received a rather disturbing e-mail," she shouted into the phone.

The young man who answered the call tried to calm her down, but she hung up after letting him know that American Widget's legal team would be hearing from her. Later that afternoon, the General Counsel was eating lunch at his desk, when he received the following e-mail. Figure 11-7 shows a transcript of the message (including punctuation errors).

To: General.Counsel@americanwidget.com

From: Hollywooddirector@studiopictures.com

Subject: FW: Account History - American Widget

Dear General Counsel of American Widget,

I received this message today. It seems someone has leaked my account history with you and I face severe reputational and financial damage. I forwarded a copy to my attorney who shall be in touch.

Please see the attached history of your purchases at American Widget. This pattern during a time of crisis in our country with so many in need of basic services shows how superficial all you Hollywood types are. You spent over $10 million to install these items in your houses around the world and millions more to maintain them. In public you talk about politicians needing to be for the working man, yet you spend all this money with a company that lays off thousands of workers to manufacture outside the U.S. Sickening. The only way to get over this illness is with a donation to the cause for $5 million.

Figure 11-7. *A snapshot of the e-mail received by the General Counsel from the Hollywood director*

The General Counsel quickly got the CEO and CFO on the phone and briefed them on the situation.

The Second Incident Response

It was just after 3 p.m. when the CIO, CISO, General Counsel, Vice-President of Sales, CFO, and CEO gathered around the large table in the boardroom. The General Counsel filled in the CIO and CISO about the events regarding the Hollywood director's e-mail.

"How do we find out who leaked the account history?" the CEO asked, looking at the CIO and CISO.

The VP of Sales spoke up, "The application we use to manage our customer experience tracks all activity in each account. We feel it is imperative to understand everyone who talks to or performs any service for our customers. It helps create the sense of a personal touch."

"It also wouldn't hurt to get our hands on a copy of the original e-mail. Maybe we could examine the headers and see if they offer any clues about who sent it," the CISO added.

"Okay, let's get started," the CEO said.

The CISO's Office

The Information Security Manager and the Security Analyst were astonished, barely able to keep their jaws from dropping, as they listened to the CISO share details of Hollywood director's e-mail. Then, the General Counsel appeared at the door.

"Two more," he said, frowning.

"Two more what?" asked the CISO.

"Two more customers are being blackmailed. The governor of a very large state and the head of an American automobile manufacturer. All with the same type of threats being made."

All four shared concerned looks, then the General Counsel left to brief the CEO on the new e-mails.

"We need to look at those accounts," the CISO said.

Log Files and a Revelation

The Information Security Manager gave the logs a cursory look: "Sales Manager is the only one in these accounts, and he is the only one with enough access to download the histories for all these people. I don't understand why he would do it."

The Security Analyst was also looking through the logs. She noticed the entries showing Sales Manager downloading the account histories to .csv files. The Information Security Manager left the room, leaving the Security Analyst to continue reviewing the logs. She accessed the governor and the automobile manufacturer's accounts and downloaded the access logs for each. She quickly observed that the histories for each account were accessed and downloaded to .csv files on the same day, at the same time: 2 a.m. She built Table 11-1, to show the others what she found.

Table 11-1. *Table Created by the Security Analyst, Listing the Activities in the Affected Accounts*

Account	User	Date	Time	Action
Hollywood Director	Sales Mgr.	5-1-2018	02:14	Download Account History
Governor	Sales Mgr.	5-1-2018	02:45	Download Account History
Auto Manufacturer	Sales Mgr.	5-1-2018	03:10	Download Account History

It was then, looking at the dates and the Sales Mgr. entry, that the Security Analyst began to get nervous. She remembered the day a few months before when she pushed the Finance Manager's laptop issues off to desktop support and the Information Security Manager wanting her to check into it. She also vaguely remembered the Information Security Manager talking about another laptop going bad the same day, that one in Sales. Her heart sank as she started going through her old e-mails. The Sales Manager's laptops exhibited the same issues as the Finance Manager's laptop on that same morning.

End Point Detection and Response (EDR)

The Security Analyst opened the EDR dashboard and navigated to the investigation screen. Entering an asset tag number for the Sales Manager's laptop, she filtered the data range a few days before and after the complaints about performance were made. After a few minutes of searching, she noticed on the day of the Sales Manager's laptop performance issues, many files were created and deleted. These actions were part of an executable downloaded and launched around 10:45 that morning. Opening another screen, she launched the investigation screen and entered the Finance Manager's laptop information. Clicking through a series of screens, she saw the same executable on Finance Manager's laptop. The same files were created and deleted. After discussing these clues with the Information Security Manager and the CISO, all three concurred that expert assistance was required.

Help Arrives

When the forensic experts arrived, seven more customers reported receiving e-mails threatening exposure if blackmail was not paid. Using the IOCs she found on the Finance Manager and Sales Manager's laptops, the Security Analyst estimated that half of the customers of American Widget had their purchase history downloaded.

The forensic investigation took several months. It was concluded that the attack focused on a well-crafted spear phishing e-mail sent to the Finance Manager. Surprisingly, the Sales Manager did not have much publicly available information for the attackers to use, so they focused on the Finance Manager. The attackers crafted an e-mail pretending to be contacts from a conference the Finance Manager had recently attended and asking for information on American Widget's products. An attachment with specifications for the proposed purchase contained an embedded executable that launched the attack.

The Information Security Manager did not understand how the ransomware attack fit into the picture. The forensic team said it was a diversion—a way to keep the team busy while account histories were downloaded and exfiltrated via DNS tunneling. The attack group that the forensic team concluded was responsible for the attack was known to work with lesser known attack groups that conducted easy-to-detect attacks that kept IR teams busy while the primary attack was under way.

Lessons Learned

Once the dust cleared, several key items were noted as issues, relating to the incident response at American Widget. At the center of the lessons learned was a lack of understanding of assets and key risk points. The Information Security Manager's focus on the locked database, not understanding that manufacturing plans are easily recoverable, left him focused on the wrong attack, allowing the attackers to successfully steal customer records. Owing to the missing risk analysis, the information security team, CISO, Information Security Manager, and all other members did not understand the impact of breached customer records. That caused the team to lose focus on the laptops of the Finance Manager and Sales Manager when issues were found.

Summary

A lack of planning and understanding can turn seemingly simple situations into full-blown catastrophes. This chapter highlighted an organization with no formalized incident response plan other than having members of an initial response team. No understanding of assets, resulting from the lack of risk analysis, caused the team to ignore potential issues with end points belonging to Sales and Finance team members. This caused the Information Security Manager to focus on the encrypted database, instead of investigating the peculiar performance issues of the compromised end points.

Conducting a risk assessment does two things:

- It leads entities to understand the most important assets the entity possesses.

- It provides a blueprint of how attackers may exploit vulnerabilities and attempt to steal, modify, or render critical assets unavailable.

Without a clear understanding of what is important to the business, the IRT cannot effectively manage the response appropriately. It is the centerpiece of building the incident response program.

CHAPTER 12

This Is a Full-Time Job

Cybersecurity, information security, whatever the title in an organization, is a large program made up of several smaller programs. Each has its own objectives and a defined strategy to meet those objectives. The incident response program is no different. Incident response seeks to identify, contain, eradicate, and recover from information security events as quickly as possible, avoiding adverse impacts to the business assets and processes targeted. The leader of the program constructs a strategy for meeting the objectives and deploys resources accordingly.

Full-Time Effort Required

The effort necessary to accomplish everything discussed throughout this book is not trivial. Strategy development, leading the team, planning, and practicing take time. Documentation from tabletop sessions, events, and incidents cannot wait. Failing to update the response plan or key playbook is an unforced error with detrimental effects during a subsequent event. Most information security pros are not solely responsible for incident response. This program must be balanced against other competing priorities. However, incident response needs must take priority over other demands of the information security program.

Building a Program

A lot of work goes into establishing and maintaining the incident response program. Proper leadership is required for success—getting the prerequisite protection capabilities established, understanding risks and potential attack vectors, preplanning for incident response by having a plan and creating the necessary playbooks. Finally, it takes practice, and a lot of it, to become proficient at responding to events and incidents.

© Eric C. Thompson 2018

Leadership

There are many everyday circumstances that are beyond the control of information security leaders and members of incident response teams: limited budgets, executives who refuse to understand the reality of cyber threats, and many other factors too numerous to mention here. Good leaders see situations for what they are and what can be done to mitigate them, refusing to think about the what ifs. Maverick McNealy, professional golfer and son of Sun Microsystems cofounder Scott McNealy, credits his father with telling him, "If you can do something about it, do it. If not, don't worry about it."[1]

Effective leadership takes work. It includes the ability to listen, stay in control of thoughts and feelings, not express every thought that comes to mind, and focus on the positives. There are always "better" tools or solutions that are badly needed by the incident response team, but not all needs can be met. In Chapter 4, Urban Meyer's leadership beliefs were discussed at length. The principles he espouses are ones all incident response leaders and information security professionals should revisit from time to time. It is not possible to control events such as, for example:

- Low budgets

- Lack of participation in incident response by management

- Gaps in preferred technology

These realities are frustrating to incident response leaders. But they cannot affect the leader's response. Figure 12-1 is a reminder of Meyer's formula.

---

[1]Ashley Mayo, "Young Maverick," *Golf Digest*, March 27, 2018.

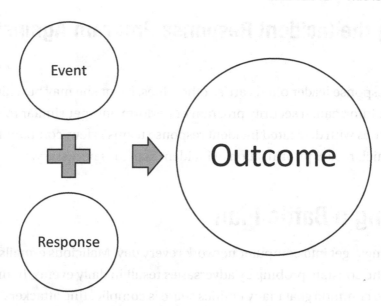

Figure 12-1. *Meyer's formula for a leader's approach to his or her circumstances*

Meyer believes that leaders cannot control events or outcomes, but the one piece of the equation under their control is response. For leaders of incident response, keeping in mind how one responds to situations affects outcomes and is controllable. Poor responses to challenging situations cause outcomes to worsen. The right response lessens the impact of challenging situations.

Continued Learning and Growth

Leaders also work on continued growth and improvement. Leaders of incident response programs must work on both their technical and leadership skills. Cybersecurity is an expansive field that is constantly changing. Threats change, exploits change, and detection methods change. Leaders must keep up on these changes. It is not necessary for them to have expertise in every competency, but leaders should know enough to enlist the help of those with the required skills and be able to spot where guidance is needed. That is the essence of building teams with the right people to get the job done. This segues into the next topic. Leaders must continue to develop their leadership skills. John Maxwell makes this point nearly every time he speaks and writes on this subject. Leaders must continue to grow, to hone the skills necessary to lead successful teams.

Balancing the Incident Response Program Against Other Priorities

The incident response leader often carries other titles. He or she may be a director or manager of the information security program or perform another similar role. The number of entities with dedicated incident response teams is few, compared to the total population, which makes prioritization of incident activities necessary.

Developing a Battle Plan

Unwanted "things" get into computer networks every day. Malicious e-mails, vulnerable software, and the constant probing by adversaries result in daily events, both major and minor. One common goal many entities share is complicating attackers' paths to targeted information assets. Anything done to make lateral movement and privilege escalation more difficult improves network and system security. Many ways of doing this are documented in articles discussing cyber hygiene. Most of these items are not related to the incident response discussion, but one topic worth discussing in relation to incident response is segmenting the network.

Network Segmentation and Incident Response

Network segmentation conjures thoughts of complexity, workload, and maintenance. It is not an easy undertaking, but it is one worth considering. If lateral movement is complicated, and opportunities for escalating privilege are fewer, attackers may decide that the effort or risk of detection is too great to continue. Flat networks, in which control of one end point presents an opportunity to compromise any other end point of an attacker's choosing, can make the attacker's task too easy. Some point to the use of vLANs as a solution to network segmentation, but only if access is somehow restricted. If every server has permission to communicate with another, this approach does not solve the problem. Two criteria are required for successful segmentation (illustrated in Figure 12-2):

- Except in exceptional circumstances, servers should not talk to other servers, and end-user devices should not talk to other end-user devices.

- vLANs and other network segments with important information assets should not allow access to any application, database, operating system, or other information system component, unless it is required as part of one's job function.

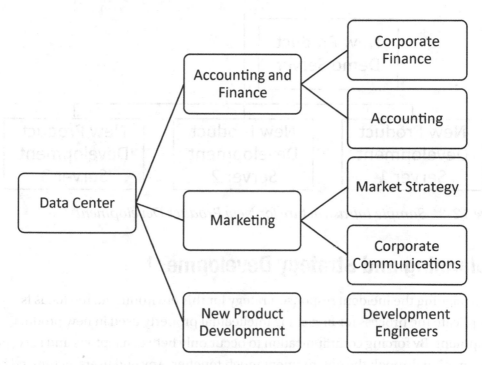

Figure 12-2. *Simple breakdown of corporate groups by function*

This figure shows a rudimentary structure for a manufacturing entity. This entity's ability to thrive depends on new product development derived by the research and development team. The concept here is to break down the end users by function: examples exist for Accounting and Finance, Marketing, and New Product Development departments.

Figure 12-3 shows a breakdown of the infrastructure within the data center for the New Product Development team. There is a production server, used when products are manufactured; a demo server for the team to use when showing executives and other stakeholders progress on new product development; and three development servers, one for each new product under development.

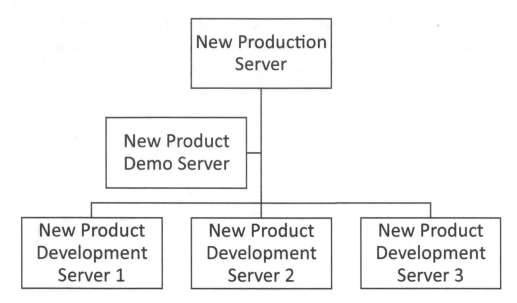

Figure 12-3. *Sample infrastructure for New Product Development*

Preplanning and Strategy Development

When designing the incident response strategy for this environment, the focus is to complicate the process for breaching intellectual property used in new product development. By forcing communication to occur only between laptops and servers, it makes pivoting through the environment much tougher. Any end users victimized by a phishing e-mail in Accounting or Marketing force the attacker to pivot between servers and laptops until a member of the development team is breached. Depending on the data targeted, controlling a laptop for someone working on New Product only has access to New Product Development Server 1. The same goes for New Product 2 and New Product 3. Production data is only accessible to the Production team. There is more work to be done by the intruder, and more opportunity to detect the intrusion.

The other value to preplanning and design of the network is understanding where ideal data collection points exist. In this environment, placing detection and traffic capture capabilities in line with communications related to all new products under development, being demonstrated, and produced is more valuable than any other internal data captures. If anything goes wrong, necessary data points to build a time line and investigate is available.

Identification

Identification is the first step in responding to events and incidents. Detective capabilities built within the entity provide the identification of events and incidents occurring within the environment. End users can detect suspicious activities and alert cybersecurity personnel, but technological capabilities provide much of the means used for identification. Entities of the smallest size often deal with large volumes of data, so much so, it becomes necessary to automate analysis and correlation. Mature security programs gather data from many sources, such as

- Applications and application servers
- Firewalls
- Intrusion detection and prevention systems
- Packet captures
- End point detection and response
- DNS security monitoring
- DLP solutions
- EDR solutions
- Infrastructure (operating systems and databases)
- Many more

Data needs a place to go and a way for analysis to occur. Security events spawn many indicators. These indicators may make obvious that an attack is occurring, and others only hint at one. The increased use of SIEM solutions was designed to identify all the subtle hints of an attack and alert cybersecurity teams. These represent just some of the capabilities organizations must implement to identify potential security incidents.

Containment

Containment requires an organization to collect indicators of compromise. Indicators are attributes and artifacts left behind during events. Threat actors have specific attributes, based on tools, techniques, and procedures used. Specific types of malware or ransomware make changes to systems the incident response team use to search the remaining information systems and assets. When matches to the indicators hit, the incident response team can quarantine those systems, taking them offline for further analysis.

The process of gathering an initial set of indicators and searching for signs of each in the remaining systems are documented in playbooks used by the response team. Playbooks are specific to event types: malware/ransomware, denial of service, lost assets, data theft, and unauthorized use or misuse of company assets. This is not a complete list but identifies very common scenarios seen by incident response teams.

During the containment phase, forensic evidence used to determine the root cause and the time line illustrating how the event unfolded is also gathered. Images of the affected systems are obtained for complete analysis of all system characteristics during containment.

During this time, incident response teams deal with contact from members of the business and company leadership who are seeking answers. This is to be expected. The organization could be impacted, depending on the severity of the events in question, and these individuals have a need to know what is occurring. The key is to give facts and not speculate. Speculation causes more harm than good.

Eradication, Recovery, and Lessons Learned

Eradication is the process of removing the malicious artifacts from the environment. It also includes mitigating vulnerabilities exploited and other weaknesses, such as those exploited by the adversary. Recovery processes place systems back into production, in a stronger state, it is hoped Updates to network hardware, additional patches, and configuration changes designed to strengthen the systems from future attacks are key. Finally, ensuring that the team sits down and goes over the event is important. This requirement is often missed. Entities do not find the time to go over the incident response process and document what is effective and what needs improvement. Common examples include updating the incident response plan or playbooks, to add or modify steps, and discussing behaviors and actions of the team, to reinforce expectations. The goal at the end of the eradication phase is to document the incident and events in an executive report outlining actions taken, outcomes, and lessons learned, with metrics tracking activities directed at desired outcomes. Ultimately, management, or the body representing management at the cybersecurity table, must review the documentation and authorize necessary changes.

Summary

Building the incident response program requires significant planning and work. Successful programs are led by strong leaders willing to associate themselves with individuals smarter than they are, if necessary, to make the response program successful. These leaders must understand the risks to critical assets; the tactics, techniques, and procedures used by attackers; and how to respond to security events. Examples of these strategic decisions and deployments include segmenting networks and deploying detection capabilities necessary to identify the presence of intruders in the network. The goal of rapid identification of bad actors targeting sensitive assets and efficiently containing and eradicating the intrusion are primary for most entities. Detecting, responding, and recovering from security events is, arguably, the most important subprogram within the information security program.

APPENDIX

NIST Cybersecurity Framework

This appendix shows each function, category, and subcategory of the National Institute of Standards and Technology's Cybersecurity Framework (NIST CSF). The functions include

- Identify
- Protect
- Detect
- Respond
- Recover

All functions contain categories, such as Asset Management, and subcategories, such as ID.AM-1, with a description. This appendix is provided as a reference to material referring to the NIST CSF when building an incident response program.

Identify: Asset Management

Table A-1 shows the Asset Management subcategories of the NIST CSF.

Table A-1. *Asset Management Subcategories*

Subcategory	Description
ID.AM-1	Physical devices and systems within the organization are inventoried.
ID.AM-2	Software platforms and applications within the organization are inventoried.
ID.AM-3	Organizational communication and data flows are mapped.
ID.AM-4	External information systems are cataloged.
ID.AM-5	Resources (e.g., hardware, devices, data, time, personnel, and software) are prioritized, based on their classification, criticality, and business value.
ID.AM-6	Cybersecurity roles and responsibilities for the entire workforce and third-party stakeholders (e.g., suppliers, customers, partners) are established.

Identify: Business Environment

Table A-2 shows the Business Environment subcategories of the NIST CSF.

Table A-2. *Business Environment Subcategories Cybersecurity Controls Mapped to the HIPAA Security Rule Safeguards*

Subcategory	Description
ID.BE-1	The organization's role in the supply chain is identified and communicated.
ID.BE-2	The organization's place in critical infrastructure and its industry sector is identified and communicated.
ID.BE-3	Priorities for organizational mission, objectives, and activities are established and communicated.
ID.BE-4	Dependencies and critical functions for delivery of critical services are established.
ID.BE-5	Resilience requirements to support delivery of critical services are established for all operating states (e.g., under duress/attack, during recovery, normal operations).

Identify: Governance

Table A-3 shows the Governance subcategories of the NIST CSF.

Table A-3. *Governance Subcategories*

Subcategory	Description
ID.GV-1	Organizational cybersecurity policy is established and communicated.
ID.GV-2	Cybersecurity roles and responsibilities are coordinated and aligned with internal roles and external partners.
ID.GV-3	Legal and regulatory requirements regarding cybersecurity, including privacy and civil liberties obligations, are understood and managed.
ID.GV-4	Governance and risk management processes address cybersecurity risks.

Identify: Risk Assessment

Table A-4 shows the Risk Assessment subcategories of the NIST CSF.

Table A-4. *Risk Assessment Subcategories*

Subcategory	Description
ID.RA-1	Asset vulnerabilities are identified and documented.
ID.RA-2	Cyber threat intelligence is received from information sharing forums and sources.
ID.RA-3	Threats, both internal and external, are identified and documented.
ID.RA-4	Potential business impacts and likelihoods are identified.
ID.RA-5	Threats, vulnerabilities, likelihoods, and impacts are used to determine risk.
ID.RA-6	Risk responses are identified and prioritized.

Identify: Risk Management

Table A-5 shows the Risk Management subcategories of the NIST CSF.

Table A-5. *Risk Management Subcategories*

Subcategory	Description
ID.RM-1	Risk management processes are established, managed, and agreed to by organizational stakeholders.
ID.RM-2	Organizational risk tolerance is determined and clearly expressed.
ID.RM-3	The organization's determination of risk tolerance is informed by its role in critical infrastructure and sector-specific risk analysis.

Identify: Supply Chain Risk Management

The organization's priorities, constraints, risk tolerances, and assumptions are established and used to support risk decisions associated with managing supply chain risk. The organization has established and implemented the processes to identify, assess, and manage supply chain risks. Table A-6 shows the Supply Chain Risk Management subcategories of the NIST CSF.

Table A-6. *Supply Chain Risk Management Subcategories*

Subcategory	Description
ID.SC-1	Cyber supply chain risk management processes are identified, established, assessed, managed, and agreed to by organizational stakeholders.
ID.SC-2	Suppliers and third-party partners of information systems, components, and services are identified, prioritized, and assessed, using a cyber supply chain risk-assessment process.
ID.SC-3	Contracts with suppliers and third-party partners are used to implement appropriate measures designed to meet the objectives of an organization's cybersecurity program and cyber supply chain risk management plan.
ID.SC-4	Suppliers and third-party partners are routinely assessed, using audits, test results, or other forms of evaluations, to confirm they are meeting their contractual obligations.
ID.SC-5	Response and recovery planning and testing are conducted with suppliers and third-party providers.

Protect: Access Control

Table A-7 shows the Access Control subcategories of the NIST CSF.

Table A-7. *Access Control Subcategories*

Subcategory	Description
PR.AC-1	Identities and credentials are issued, managed, verified, revoked, and audited for authorized devices, users, and processes.
PR.AC-2	Physical access to assets is managed and protected.
PR.AC-3	Remote access is managed.
PR.AC-4	Access permissions are managed, incorporating the principles of least privilege and separation of duties.
PR.AC-5	Network integrity is protected, incorporating network segregation, where appropriate.

Protect: Awareness and Training

Table A-8 shows the Awareness and Training subcategories of the NIST CSF.

Table A-8. *Awareness and Training Subcategories*

Subcategory	Description
PR.AT-1	All users are informed and trained.
PR.AT-2	Privileged users understand roles and responsibilities.
PR.AT-3	Third-party stakeholders (e.g., supplier's customers, partners) understand roles and responsibilities.
PR.AT-4	Senior executives understand roles and responsibilities.
PR.AT-5	Physical and information security personnel understand roles and responsibilities.

Protect: Data Security

Table A-9 shows the Data Security subcategories of the NIST CSF.

Table A-9. *Data Security Subcategories*

Subcategory	Description
PR.DS-1	Data-at-rest is protected.
PR.DS-2	Data-in-transit is protected.
PR.DS-3	Assets are formally managed throughout removal, transfers, and disposition.
PR.DS-4	Adequate capacity to ensure availability is maintained.
PR.DS-5	Protections against data leaks are implemented.
PR.DS-6	Integrity checking mechanisms are used to verify software, firmware, and information integrity.

Protect: Information Protection

Table A-10 shows the Information Protection subcategories of the NIST CSF.

Table A-10. *Information Protection Subcategories*

Subcategory	Description
PR.IP-1	A baseline configuration of information technology/industrial control systems is created and maintained.
PR.IP-2	A System Development Life Cycle to manage systems is implemented.
PR.IP-3	Configuration change control processes are in place.
PR.IP-4	Backups of information are conducted, maintained, and tested periodically.
PR.IP-5	Policy and regulations regarding the physical operating environment for organizational assets are met.
PR.IP-6	Data is destroyed according to policy.
PR.IP-7	Protection processes are continuously improved.
PR.IP-8	Effectiveness of protection technologies is shared with appropriate parties.
PR.IP-9	Response plans (Incident Response and Business Continuity) and recovery plans (Incident Recovery and Disaster Recovery) are in place and managed.
PR.IP-10	Response and recovery plans are tested.
PR.IP-11	Cybersecurity is included in human resources practices (e.g., deprovisioning, personnel screening).
PR.IP-12	A vulnerability management plan is developed and implemented.

Protect: Maintenance

Table A-11 shows the Maintenance subcategories of the NIST CSF.

Table A-11. *Maintenance Subcategories*

Subcategory	Description
PR.MA-1	Maintenance and repair of organizational assets is performed and logged in a timely manner, with approved and controlled tools.
PR.MA-2	Remote maintenance of organizational assets is approved, logged, and performed in a manner that prevents unauthorized access.

Protect: Protective Technology

Table A-12 shows the Protective Technology subcategories of the NIST CSF.

Table A-12. *Protective Technology Subcategories*

Subcategory	Description
PR.PT-1	Audit/log records are determined, documented, implemented, and reviewed, in accordance with policy.
PR.PT-2	Removable media is protected, and its use restricted, according to policy.
PR.PT-3	Access to systems and assets is controlled, incorporating the principle of least functionality.
PR.PT-4	Communications and control networks are protected.

Detect: Anomalies and Events

Table A-13 shows the Anomalies and Events subcategories of the NIST CSF.

Table A-13. *Anomalies and Events Subcategories*

Subcategory	Description
DE.AE-1	A baseline of network operations and expected data flows for users and systems is established and managed.
DE.AE-2	Detected events are analyzed to understand attack targets and methods.
DE.AE-3	Event data are aggregated and correlated from multiple sources and sensors.
DE.AE-4	Impact of events is determined.
DE.AE-5	Incident alert thresholds are established.

Detect: Continuous Monitoring

Table A-14 shows the Continuous Monitoring subcategories of the NIST CSF.

Table A-14. *Continous Monitoring Subcategories*

Subcategory	Description
DE.CM-1	The network is monitored to detect potential cybersecurity events.
DE.CM-2	The physical environment is monitored to detect potential cybersecurity events.
DE.CM-3	Personnel activity is monitored to detect potential cybersecurity events.
DE.CM-4	Malicious code is detected.
DE.CM-5	Unauthorized mobile code is detected.
DE.CM-6	External service provider activity is monitored to detect potential cybersecurity events.
DE.CM-7	Monitoring for unauthorized personnel, connections, devices, and software is performed.
DE.CM-8	Vulnerability scans are performed.

Detect: Detection Processes

Table A-15 shows the Detection Processes subcategories of the NIST CSF.

Table A-15. *Detection Processes Subcategories*

Subcategory	Description
DE.DP-1	Roles and responsibilities for detection are well defined to ensure accountability.
DE.DP-2	Detection activities comply with all applicable requirements.
DE.DP-3	Detection processes are tested.
DE.DP-4	Event detection Information is communicated to appropriate parties.
DE.DP-5	Detection processes are continuously improved.

Respond: Response Planning

Table A-16 shows the Response Planning subcategories of the NIST CSF.

Table A-16. *Response Planning Subcategories*

Subcategory	Description
RS.RP-1	Response plan is executed during or after an incident.

Respond: Communications

Table A-17 shows the Communications subcategories of the NIST CSF.

Table A-17. *Communications Subcategories.*

Subcategory	Description
RS.CO-1	Personnel know their roles and order of operations when a response is needed.
RS.CO-2	Events are reported consistent with established criteria.
RS.CO-3	Information is shared consistent with response plans.
RS.CO-4	Coordination with stakeholders occurs consistent with response plans.
RS.CO-5	Voluntary information sharing occurs with external stakeholders to achieve broader cybersecurity situational awareness.

Respond: Analysis

Table A-18 shows the Analysis subcategories of the NIST CSF.

Table A-18. *Analysis Subcategories*

Subcategory	Description
RS.AN-1	Notifications from detection systems are investigated.
RS.AN-2	The impact of the incident is understood.
RS.AN-3	Forensics are performed.
RS.AN-4	Incidents are categorized consistent with response plans.

Respond: Mitigation

Table A-19 shows the Mitigation subcategories of the NIST CSF.

Table A-19. *Mitigation Subcategories*

Subcategory	Description
RS.MI-1	Incidents are contained.
RS.MI-2	Incidents are mitigated.
RS.MI-3	Newly identified vulnerabilities are mitigated or documented as accepted risks.

Respond: Improvement

Table A-20 shows the Improvement subcategories of the NIST CSF.

Table A-20. *Improvement Subcategories*

Subcategory	Description
RS.IM-1	Response plans incorporate lessons learned.
RS.IM-2	Response strategies are updated.

Recover: Recovery Planning

Table A-21 shows the Recovery Planning subcategories of the NIST CSF.

Table A-21. *Recovery Planning Subcategories*

Subcategory	Description
RC.RP-1	Recovery plan is executed during or after an event.

Recover: Improvements

Table A-22 shows the Improvements subcategories of the NIST CSF.

Table A-22. *Improvements Subcategories*

Subcategory	Description
RC.IM-1	Recovery plans incorporate lessons learned.
RC.IM-2	Recovery strategies are updated

Recover: Communications

Table A-23 shows the Communications subcategories of the NIST CSF.

Table A-23. *Communications Subcategories*

Subcategory	Description
RC.CO-1	Public relations are managed.
RC.CO-2	Reputation after an event is repaired.
RC.CO-3	Recovery activities are communicated to internal stakeholders and executive and management teams.

Index

A, B

Breach, 65, 66, 68, 70

C

Command and control (C2), 109
Continuous monitoring
    analyzing data, 125, 133, 134
    reporting, 125, 133, 134
    security controls, 128, 129, 131, 132, 135
    strategy, 125, 126, 128, 129, 132, 133
Culture, 4, 9, 10
    cybersecurity and incident
        response, 54
    leadership skills, 55
    team skills, 56
    technical skills, 55, 56
Cyber risks
    activities, 72
    analysis, 71
    measurement
        impact, 76, 77
        likelihood, 75–77
    review, 77
    risk register, 77, 78
    threat analysis, 73, 74
    vulnerabilities, 74, 75
Cybersecurity functions
    incident response support, 15
Cybrary, 55

D

Data loss prevention (DLP), 87–90, 98
Data theft, 99, 113, 114, 116
Decisiveness, 51
Denial of service (DoS), 112, 118

E, F, G

Emotional intelligence, 52, 53
End point detection and response (EDR),
    87, 91, 98, 147
End users, 82
Equifax, 83
Event, 65–70
Event and response phases, 68, 69

H

Humility, 48, 50

I, J

Incident, 65–70
Incident handling, 17, 28, 30, 32–33
Incident response, 1–10, 57
    containment, 157
    eradication and recovery, 158
    goals, 67
    identification, 157
    leadership, 152, 153

Printed in the United States
By Bookmasters